A PLUME BOOK

THE CAT WHO CAME BACK FOR CHRISTMAS

JULIA ROMP lives in Isleworth with her son, George, and their cat, Ben. When she is not looking after her family and the stray cats in the area, Julia works for the charity Lost and Found helping to re-home cats. After the success of her campaign to find Ben, Julia has become known as the local pet detective.

Praise for *The Cat Who Came Back for Christmas*

"Ben went so far as to change the lives of his owners. . . . It's a gripping story we know you'll love." —*Your Cat* Magazine

"The heartwarming true story of how a cat changed a little boy's life . . . A very interesting read which is both uplifting and informative." —*South Wales Argus*

"A sheer delight . . . a truly inspirational autobiography." —*Cork Evening Echo*

"The incredibly moving story of how George found salvation in a loyal pet." —*International Express* (London)

The Cat Who Came Back for Christmas

HOW A CAT BROUGHT A FAMILY THE GIFT OF LOVE

Julia Romp

A PLUME BOOK

PLUME

Published by Penguin Group

Penguin Group (USA) Inc., 375 Hudson Street, New York, New York 10014, U.S.A. •
Penguin Group (Canada), 90 Eglinton Avenue East, Suite 700, Toronto, Ontario,
Canada M4P 2Y3 (a division of Pearson Penguin Canada Inc.) • Penguin Books
Ltd., 80 Strand, London WC2R 0RL, England • Penguin Ireland, 25 St. Stephen's
Green, Dublin 2, Ireland (a division of Penguin Books Ltd.) • Penguin Group
(Australia), 250 Camberwell Road, Camberwell, Victoria 3124, Australia (a
division of Pearson Australia Group Pty. Ltd.) • Penguin Books India Pvt.
Ltd., 11 Community Center, Panchsheel Park, New Delhi – 110 017, India •
Penguin Books (NZ), 67 Apollo Drive, Rosedale, Auckland 0632, New Zealand
(a division of Pearson New Zealand Ltd.) • Penguin Books (South Africa) (Pty.)
Ltd., 24 Sturdee Avenue, Rosebank, Johannesburg 2196, South Africa

Penguin Books Ltd., Registered Offices: 80 Strand, London WC2R 0RL, England

First published by Plume, a member of Penguin Group (USA) Inc. Previously
published in the United Kingdom by HarperCollins as *A Friend Like Ben*.

First American Printing, October 2012
10   9   8   7   6   5   4

CIP data is available.

ISBN 978-0-452-29878-1

Printed in the United States of America

For George, who opened my eyes to your world and what a wonderful place it can be, and in loving memory of my dad, Colin, who gave me the laughter that I try to pass on to George every day

Prologue

When it came to first impressions, Ben didn't exactly shine. He wasn't a small, pretty kitten with a blaze of ginger hair or even a sleek adult cat with a shining tortoiseshell coat. In fact, his black and white fur was covered in dried blood, his red rump was completely bare and his thin tail looked more like a hairy twig. Thankfully, I couldn't tell by looking at him that he was also home to scores of fleas and ear mites.

But as off-putting as he looked, when the sickly stray started visiting my garden I left out food, because I've always been soft when it comes to animals. Even my pet rabbit Fluffy lives in a shed that I painted with bright flowers—it's like the Ritz for rabbits—so I made up a bed for the cat in a carrier, which I left in the shed, hoping it would sleep there. The stray was looking worse each day and, I thought, once it felt at home in the carrier, I'd shut the door and take it to the vet.

Please let him be sleeping, I'd think each morning as I walked up the garden with my ten-year-old son, George, to check if the food had been eaten or whether the blanket had been disturbed.

Together we'd peer into the back of the dark shed and see the cat's eyes peeping out at us. They were light, acid green, like the first leaves on a lime tree in spring, and every time I saw them, they stopped me in my tracks for just a moment. But although the cat was sometimes sitting on a shelf or sometimes next to a flowerpot, it was never in the cage.

"Boo!" George would say as he tried to play hide and seek with the cat whenever we went to see it, and I was glad because he didn't often play games with anyone.

Autism made George's world a very lonely place at times and other children found him almost as inexplicable as he found them. They were afraid of the rage which burst out of him in screams and shouts, while he was just as frightened by the noises they made and the way they jostled him in the school corridor. That's why it was good to see George take an interest in the cat, even though the cat didn't take an interest back. Whenever George or I went too near it, the cat would hiss and spit, its teeth bared and fur coat spring-ing to attention. It obviously didn't want anything to do with either of us.

But time and good food can do powerful things to animals, just like they can to people. Slowly the stray got comfortable enough to start sleeping in the carrier bed, and after another few more weeks, I managed to shut the door with a broom handle.

When I took the cat to the vet, I explained that I wasn't its official owner and left the cat in their care, telling myself my job was done. I'd put up posters in the local area with a picture of the stray, and if anyone came forward, I would put them in touch with the vet. But no one did, and a few weeks later came the call I'd been secretly dreading.

"Would you give the cat a home?" the vet asked, and I didn't know what to say. Now, if you knew me, you'd know how unusual that is. My mum says the phrase "talk the hind legs off a donkey" was invented for me and she's right. But I was lost for words when the vet asked me about the cat, because on the one hand I loved animals, and on the other I'd vowed never to have a cat because my childhood home had been so full of them that there was hardly space for me. Besides, although George had seemed interested in the stray, we hadn't had much success with animals, because he found it hard to bond with anything. Polly the budgie had had to be re-homed because its noise disturbed George, and he'd quickly lost interest in Fluffy the rabbit. It wasn't his fault. George just didn't connect with things the way other children did—however much I wished he would—and I didn't want to take on anything else, because it was such a full-time job looking after him.

But as I hesitated, the vet suggested that maybe we could just pay the cat a visit.

"He seems sad," he said. "I think he'd like to see a friendly face."

What could I do? My heart won over my head and I took George to the vet's, where we saw a familiar ball of black and white fur curled up in a cage. Then it stood up, and I saw that the cat had a huge shaved patch on its stomach and a plastic collar around its neck to stop it worrying its stitches. It looked even uglier than it had before, but that didn't seem to put George off in the slightest as he knelt down beside the cage.

"Benny Boo!" he said in a high voice I'd never heard before, sounding expectant, excited.

"Is you feeling better now, Ben?" George asked. "Is you well?" Again, he spoke in a singsong voice I didn't recognize, and the cat meowed back as he talked to it.

"I think he likes you," the veterinary nurse who'd shown us into the room said with a smile.

George immediately went silent. He didn't like talking to anyone, let alone strangers, and he couldn't look people in the eye if they tried to speak to him; instead he stared silently past them at something in the distance, anywhere other than in their eyes. But as soon as the nurse busied herself with something else and George knew he wasn't being watched, he bent down to the cage once again.

"Benny Boo!" he said in his high voice. "Is your tummy hurting?"

He pressed his face even closer to the bars of the cage and I started moving forward, sure that the cat would claw at him through the bars, just as it had whenever we'd gone to see it in the shed. But then I stopped because, as the cat looked solemnly at George, it stepped carefully forward before turning its body against the length of the cage and rubbing up against the bars. Where had the hissing, spitting cat we knew so well gone? I thought I was seeing things. Then I decided I was hearing them when the stray started making a throaty, rolling purr as it moved in time with the words George was speaking to it.

"Ben, Ben!" he chanted. "Is you well now? Is you well?"

The cat sniffed the air and George bent down even closer to it. As his head drew level with the cat's, it looked him square in the eyes and I was sure he would turn away. But George didn't. Instead of staring past the cat or hanging his head, he stared right back at the cat. The two of them did not break eye contact for a second as George carried on talking softly. I held my breath, looking at the two of them in shock: George talking to the cat and smiling as though it was something he did every day, the cat staring back with its green eyes full of something I can only describe as acceptance. It looked like an old soul who's seen it all and is surprised by nothing.

Well, I knew what I had to do, didn't I? Like they say, hope springs eternal. I didn't know why George liked the cat—maybe it was just a moment in one day or maybe it was the fact that he knew the world would have a hard time accepting the strange-looking animal, just as it did him. But I'd seen a glimmer of something that I'd spent George's whole lifetime longing to see him show another living thing: love. And the cat seemed to feel just as strongly about him. That was enough for me. All I hoped back then was that the cat might become a friend for George. What I could never have known was that it would change our lives forever—in more ways than I could have ever thought possible.

PART ONE

Before Ben

Chapter 1

London is a global city, but it can still be very small if you are born and brought up there. Away from the royal palaces and parks, skyscrapers and museums, red buses hooting around corners and pedestrians jostling for space on busy streets, are places where you know your neighbors and where the streets you walked on as a child don't look so very different when you finally grow up. That's the kind of place I was born in: one of London's western outer boroughs called Hounslow, where families who had been there for generations mixed with others who'd arrived more recently and where everyone knew each other by sight at least, if not from a chat over the garden fence.

London, you see, isn't just made up of the mansions and skyscrapers printed on postcards. These are few and far between by the time you get a few miles out of the center of the city. There instead are rows and rows of terraced houses battling for space with tower blocks, and while some areas get smartened up, there are a lot that don't. Hounslow, where I grew up, wasn't the poshest of places but it wasn't the roughest either. We lived on an estate built in the 1930s in one half of a semi with my nan and granddad, Doris and George, next door. I was born in 1973, the decade of flared trousers, the Bee Gees and skateboarding—like a more up-to-date Austin Powers film but for real—and while many people say this, I know for sure that mine was a truly happy childhood.

There were six of us at home: my mum, Carol, who looked after us all; my dad, Colin, who drove a black London taxi for a living; my older sister, Victoria; and our younger brothers, Colin and Andrew. Not that anyone knew us by our names, of course. Victoria was known as Tor, Colin was Boy, Andrew was Nob (weird, I know; I have no idea where that one came from) and I was Ju. We didn't ever question why we didn't go by our proper names, because we didn't question anything. Our life together was as comfortable as an old pair of slippers.

Back then, it was different for kids to how it is today. At weekends and during the school holidays, we had left the house by 9:00 a.m. and we only went back for a bit of lunch or to get a plaster on a cut knee. Tor, Boy, Nob and I played in the local parks with our friends, where there was always someone to keep an eye on us. The worst trouble usually involved falling out over a water fight and the best noise of any day was the sound of the ice-cream van. On high days and holidays, my dad would pile us into his cab and whizz us into town, where he'd drive us up the Mall to watch the changing of the guards at Buckingham Palace or down the Embankment to the Tower of London. On more run-of-the-

mill days, we'd go in to see Nan and Granddad or up to
M___'s allotment, where she grew all our veggies on a patch
army barracks.

tea?" Mum would ask after what
d she'd pour us all a cuppa from
ith her.

to love milkshakes early and
atered-down wine, British chil-
a soaked into their bones from
re out the cradle. Tea was the
ife's setbacks, according to my
f tea like one of those I'd had as a
hen I'd dreamed of fixing up the
alamity Jane, was poured once
t 16 and we all wondered what I'd
got on at school because I was a
ers had said again and again that
just before I left, I did work expe-
nd a whole new world opened up
rk, was good at something for a
for the day. I couldn't wait to leave

did, after a chat over a cuppa with
w years later they poured another
ed to marry me. I'd met him when I
er shop, where I was on the phone
local undertaker, Alan, who was on
to the vicar, Harry. Funerals, just
like weddings, are important business to any florist, but
when I made up wreaths I liked to think I was also helping
grieving families say a proper goodbye. Then at the end of a

busy day, I'd meet up with Alan and Harry, who weren't much older than me, and we'd go out.

"Aren't you the florist, undertaker and vicar?" people would ask, looking really surprised that three people so used to the sad business of giving the dead a good send-off could enjoy themselves. We were even spotted in the local disco a few times, and we all laughed when people's mouths dropped open in surprise. I liked Harry more and more as I got to know him. He was kind and considerate, and never judged anyone who came through the doors of the church youth club he ran and where I volunteered. He had all the time in the world for everybody—day and night—and I liked that.

Trouble was, though, I was totally unprepared when he asked my dad if he could marry me. I thought Harry was just coming round for tea, but he only went and told Dad that he wanted to pop the question, didn't he? I was young, about 20 at the time, and couldn't believe it. I'd always dreamed of having what my parents did, but I wasn't ready just yet. I burst into tears of surprise when Harry spoke to Dad because I didn't want to leave my lovely, comfortable home. Most of my friends still lived with their parents and I liked the way things were.

"Let's have a cuppa, Ju," my dad said after Harry had left.

The vicar had got the message that maybe I wasn't ready to be his wife when I'd started crying, and I wasn't the only one who'd been surprised by his proposal. Dad had laughed out loud when Harry spoke to him and I think he was almost as shocked as I was that anyone would think I could make a wife, because I was still so young and dizzy.

smelling of talcum powder.

When they brought George back a few minutes later, the nurses suggested giving him a bottle of water and Mum took the baby because I was still so shaky I didn't trust myself to hold him. But as he was lowered into Mum's arms George just carried on screaming, and as I looked at them together I could see she was struggling to feed him. I wondered how I was ever going to do it if Mum couldn't. She was an expert after four children, but even she was having trouble.

"He'll learn," Mum said with a smile as she looked at George wrapped up in his blanket, his face red and blotchy from wailing. "These things take time, but it will come naturally. Don't worry, Ju."

I didn't know it then, of course, but this was something I would hear again and again over the weeks, months and years that followed. Mum was only being kind, but hers was the first of a thousand explanations about George.

"His hips are a bit stiff, so he might be a bit uncomfortable," one nurse said as he screamed and screamed in the days after he was born.

"It was quite a difficult delivery, so he needs time to settle," another told me.

I'd be a rich woman today if I had a pound for every time I heard the words "It will take time." Back then I believed what I was told and was sure George would be calmer when I took him home. I'd read all the books and knew that some babies take a while to adjust to life. He'd settle when he was surrounded by love and warmth instead of a clinical hospital ward. But even when we got home to Hounslow and I started giving George warm baths or putting him in his pram, walking him up and down the garden, draping him over my shoulder, laying him on his back or rocking him in a bouncy chair, nothing calmed him.

You see, I loved George from the moment I saw him and wanted to do my best for him. He was my baby, a tiny, defenseless creature I had created and would be responsible for forever; a part of me that I would do anything to love and protect. But as the days turned into weeks, I began to feel as if he didn't want the love and care I had to give him. It might sound silly to say that about a tiny baby, but George would scream even louder whenever I went near him and I just didn't understand it because I thought babies loved to be cuddled.

When the midwife visited, she said that I should take him to the doctor, who referred me to the local hospital, who said George might be suffering from constipation and gave him some medication. But still he didn't stop crying. Then the midwife suggested that massage might help, but George went rigid the moment I touched him, as if the feel of my hands burned his skin. Later he'd lift his head when my skin made contact with his and jerk the moment I touched him. It was the same if I tried to calm him by rocking him or laying him against my chest. He just didn't want to be close to me and screamed night and day.

Each day I told myself that things would get better, but they didn't. I hung a mobile over George's cot, thinking he'd like the bright colors, but he stared past it. I wiggled brightly colored toys in front of his face, but he turned away and cried. The hardest thing was his sleeplessness, because he would only nap for half an hour at most; day and night, he was awake.

I could see my kindly midwife thought I might be being impatient when I told her he didn't rest. "All babies sleep," she said. "It's important that they do."

But George didn't.

"He'll have to drop off in the end," Mum would tell me. "He's been fed, he's warm and he's got a clean nappy. He'll go to sleep."

But George's screams would echo around the house all night as people tried to sleep. Our home had four bedrooms: Tor was in one, Nob in another, and both had to get up for work every morning. Then there were George and me in the third, and Mum and Dad had the last one with my nephew Lewis, who was three and a half. My brother Boy and his girlfriend, Sandra, had had Lewis when they were only teenagers and were too young to cope when he was born at just 22 weeks, weighing two and a half pounds. Lewis was christened during his first few hours in the hospital because the doctors didn't think he'd survive, but he did. He came home nine months later to be looked after by Mum and Dad, because he still had such bad lung problems that he needed permanent oxygen, which is why he still slept in their room so that he could be checked every hour. George's screams meant no one was getting any sleep though, and it's one thing trying to calm an unhappy baby but another when you're worrying about everyone else too. So I started staying in my room more during the day, because I thought that at least people would get a bit of a break then with a couple of walls between them and George's cries.

"Don't worry, Ju," Dad would say as he opened the door to see me holding the baby, who'd gone rigid and red as I lifted him up. "It'll be all right. He'll grow out of it."

On days when Mum could see I'd just about reached the end of my tether, she'd strap Lewis into one side of the backseat of her car while I put George in the other and we'd go out for a drive, hoping the rhythm might send him to sleep. Hounslow is just a couple of miles from Richmond Park, a huge green space where Charles I took his court to escape the plague. It's a beautiful place and we often went there for a picnic or a walk, so it held many happy memories for me. But all those seemed to fade as we drove through the park with George screaming.

"He'll be fine," Mum would tell me. "Some babies just take a while to adjust. Things always get better."

But as I stared at packs of deer running across the park with the skyline of inner London far in the distance, I began to wonder if they ever would.

Chapter 2

Even when you live on £85 a week you can still afford a tin of paint, so that's what I bought when I moved into my own flat with George, because I wanted to brighten up the place. I had left Mum and Dad's, because families are a bit like balloons, in that they'll expand and expand to fit, but there comes a point when too much pressure might make them pop. I knew that everyone I loved was getting stressed by George, however much they didn't want to tell me. So by the time he was six months old, I had decided to put my name down on the council housing list, because our house was packed to the rafters.

Mum didn't just have Lewis to worry about now, either. My dad had developed rheumatoid arthritis when I was a teenager, but I hadn't known then just how much his illness affected him because my parents never hinted at their problems in front of us. I thought life was perfect as I sat on the sofa watching *Superman*. But as I got older, I could see for myself just how much Dad was suffering. By the time I got pregnant he had given up full-time work, though he still sometimes had huge steroid injections to stop the pain long enough for him to get out of bed and into a cab to earn a few quid. But even that had stopped when I brought George home. By then Dad's hands had curled in on themselves like claws, his back was arched and he had to use a stick to walk.

That was why I knew I had to get a place of my own, however much I hated the thought of being a single mother living on handouts, and in January 1997 I was given the keys to a two-bedroom house on an estate a couple of miles away. I arrived with a pram, a bed, a fridge and cooker Mum and Dad had bought me and a sofa covered in blue cord. I was happy to find the house immaculate. The old man called Bob who'd lived and died there had kept it well—if I heard once from the neighbors that he'd haunt me if I didn't keep his woodwork nice then I heard it a thousand times. But even Bob's neatness couldn't hide the fact that there was a bare concrete floor and I could have grown mushrooms in the darkened rooms.

I knew what Mum and Dad were thinking when they dropped me off: as sad as they were to see me go, I was an adult and had made my choices. Now I had to live with them, and while I knew they were right, I still wanted to chase after them as they drove off and beg them to take me back home. I just could not believe that this was actually real. It was a world away from all the dreams I'd had.

Even though my new house was dark, I could make it colorful at least. Bob might have kept everything neat, but he was too fond of magnolia walls for my liking. So, with my family's help, I painted the living room yellow, the corridors light green and my bedroom pink. I didn't go near the wallpaper covering the walls of the back bedroom, though. It was so old it must have been worth something and was covered in huge blue psychedelic flowers. I'd have had to do a hundred coats to cover it up and couldn't face being trapped in the room while I tried to transform it.

The new coat of paint in the rest of the flat definitely raised my spirits, as did the fact that Howard and his mum lived nearby. Even though Howard and I were no longer together, I wanted George to know his father and I'd take him to see his dad and grandma Zena. I also visited Mum and Dad every day because I was glad of the company. But although I saw people and tried to make the best of things, life didn't get any easier with George, and looking back I realize those first few months with him alone were the time when I began learning to hide my worries. You can't keep moaning, can you, bursting into tears when people ask how you are and all you want to do is cry? I could have told them my life felt like a nightmare: I was alone with a baby who cried day in, day out, and who at times felt like a visitor I could not make happy instead of my own child. But it wouldn't have done any good, so I didn't.

Besides, I was sure the reason George wasn't happy was that I was making a mess of things. I could see for myself that other women did a much better job than I did. Watching their babies smile or gurgle at them, I longed for George to do the same. But he didn't want to shake rattles or be cuddled, and when I took him back to the doctor the answer was always the same.

"It's your first child," he would say. "Don't worry so much, Julia. You're a great mum. Just relax a bit and the baby will too."

So after being told I was worrying about nothing a hundred times, I pushed down the voice inside that was telling me something was wrong; it's amazing just how much you can kid yourself. Each night when I tried to get George to sleep, knowing it would be hours before he dropped off, I'd tell myself that things would improve the next day. Each morning when he woke up and started crying, I'd vow that I just had to get through this one because tomorrow was another day. Scarlett O'Hara didn't have a patch on me when she grubbed in the dirt outside Tara.

Sometimes, though, after days of George's crying I'd feel so close to breaking point that I'd leave him in an upstairs bedroom to wail. Closing the door, I'd go downstairs just to be away from the noise, and guilt would fill me that I wasn't giving George the happiness that I'd had as a child. I knew it wasn't the same for him to have a mum at home and a dad who lived down the road, and his cries were his way of telling me that I just wasn't enough. But then I'd go back upstairs, look at George in his cot, so small and perfect with his round, chubby cheeks and puff of blond hair, and wonder what kind of mother I was. Bit by bit, I shut myself away as I started to hide both George and myself from the world, and our tiny house began to feel like a prison.

The estate where we were living didn't exactly help keep up my spirits either. There's good and bad everywhere, from the Hollywood Hills to the slums of India, but let's just say there was a lot more bad than I was used to where I was living now. Shouts would echo at night as people argued, and I'd hear the smack of punches thrown in drunken fights. Or there'd be a knock on the door as one of the stream of men who hired out one of my neighbors by the hour mistook my house for hers. The gray concrete estate looked like a jail and some of the people living there knew that from experience.

It was then that I also saw for the first time just how much drugs affect some lives. I'd never even had a cigarette, but now I saw people with eyes that were blank and desperate at the same time. Most days there would be a knock on the door and I'd open it to find someone offering to sell me wrinkle cream or baby clothes, whatever they'd managed to steal in the hope of getting whatever they could for it in order to pay for a fix.

I hated being in the pathway of all the trouble, and so six months after moving on to the estate I leaped at the chance to swap my house for a second-floor flat in another block. So what if the ceiling was covered in nicotine stains and the front door didn't lock? I could see blue sky outside my windows and soon made my first friend on the estate—a woman called Jane, who came to introduce herself one day after Dad, who had taken enough steroids to fell a horse so that his hands would work long enough, put on a new front door with Nob's help.

"Don't go answering the bell at night," Jane told me as we had a cup of tea. "Just keep yourself to yourself and you'll be fine."

Jane was tall and slim, and I never saw her without full makeup and a pair of high stilettos. She always looked as if she was about to be whisked off to Harvey Nichols in a limousine instead of going up Hounslow high street. She seemed to like keeping an eye on me and so did her boyfriend, Martin, who was just as kind. Sometimes he would appear at the door with a slice off one of the pig's heads they cooked in a pot, which I took with a heavy heart because I didn't like to tell Martin that I was vegetarian. Those were the kind of people he and Jane were: kind and generous, good neighbors who kept an eye on me and did whatever they could to help. Yes, I quickly realized they had a bit of a liking for Diamond White, but it didn't worry me because who was I to judge? As a single mum on a council estate without a penny to her name, there wasn't exactly much for me to get uppity about.

George was sitting beside Lewis in front of the television at Mum and Dad's house.

"Look at the two of them, Ju," she said with a smile.

Lewis and George were watching *Tots TV*, just as they always did, because neither of them could get enough of the three rag dolls called Tilly, Tom and Tiny.

"He's a good boy, isn't he, love?" Mum said as she looked at George, who'd got up to follow Lewis out of the room now the program had ended.

It was 1998. George was two and he'd started walking and crawling just as he should have done a few months after his first birthday. A year on he followed Lewis around like a shadow and my mum and dad were still trying to encourage me with him. I didn't say too much when they did. I knew everyone was being kind, but I was beginning to feel sure that my problems with George weren't just of my own making because although I did everything I could to make him happy, it was like living with a stranger. He could change from happy to raging in the blink of an eye and as much as everyone tried to pretend that normal rules applied to George, I knew they didn't.

Take sleeping. At night George would lie awake in his cot for hours, and the moment he learned how to climb out of it, he'd get up every few minutes and scream without stopping if I tried putting him back down. It wasn't that I was afraid of his temper or making rules. But I could see in George's eyes that he just didn't understand what I was trying to teach him. So I had no other choice but to let him toddle around the flat until he finally fell into an exhausted sleep. We must have walked a fair few marathons doing laps of our tiny flat, and even when I did get him into his cot, he often lay awake, chanting words and phrases over and over.

"Buzz Lightyear, Buzz Lightyear, Buzz Lightyear," he'd say again and again, because those were two of the handful of words that he used now, along with "Dad," "Mum" or "Batman."

"It's just not possible," the doctor would tell me when I went to see him, almost beside myself. "Everyone needs to sleep—especially children."

"But George doesn't."

The doctor looked at me with a slight smile. "I think you must have fallen asleep yourself, Julia, so you didn't realize that George had as well."

I knew I hadn't, but I was learning to keep quiet, and although I still took George to the doctor when something new happened, because I wanted to make sure there wasn't an obvious health problem, I didn't keep asking questions when I was told he was fine. I'd been brought up to trust doctors, after all, and everyone kept telling me his behavior was down to me.

That's why I was doing everything I could to make a better life for us and had signed up to do the Knowledge, the exams that license people to become London cab drivers. I wanted to go back to work and provide for George, so I'd been studying every spare moment for the past eighteen months, with Dad encouraging me. "Driving a cab would be the perfect job for you, Ju," he'd tell me. "You can study for the Knowledge at home and then go to work when it suits you, just like I did."

But, like a lot of things in life, learning the Knowledge was easier said than done. Driving for a living might sound simple, but if you want to pick up passengers in central London you have to memorize all the streets within a 6-mile radius of Charing Cross station near Trafalgar Square—and there are 25,000 of them. Training for the Knowledge is so hard it's been proved to make your brain grow, and it doesn't just end at learning the streets one by one. You also have to know the "runs." These are set routes that get you from any A to any B—lists of streets so long that they fill entire books. I wasn't sure my brain could fit all that in, and the other big problem was that I hated driving in central London.

"Faster, Ju, faster," Dad would shout when I took him up the Great West Road in his old silver Mustang.

But as soon as I pressed my foot on the accelerator and felt the massive old car almost take off, I'd slow down again in fright. I was too slow for central London, so I decided to study for a suburban license, which would allow me to pick up passengers in the suburb that included Hounslow. It would still mean memorizing thousands of streets, though, so after having an interview and being accepted to train for the Knowledge, I began studying for it at home with George. Putting him in a bouncy chair, I'd sit down surrounded by maps and stare at them as I tried to memorize the roads and runs while he cried fit to burst.

"New Brentford cemetery to Hounslow railway station," I'd chant to myself. "Left Sutton Lane, forward Wellington Road, left Staines Road, right Hibernia Road, left Hanworth Road, right Heath Road, right Whitton Road, pull up on the left on Station Road. You are now at your destination."

That was an easy one, mind; there were up to 50 streets in some of the runs. But in a strange way having something else to concentrate on made it easier to cope with George. I'd check that his nappy was dry, he was warm and his tummy was full, and he would still scream; but as I looked at his tiny red face, I'd tell myself that the Knowledge was going to get us out of this life. When I passed it and started working, I would earn enough money to get us a better one. Somehow I had to give that to George, because as he got older, his behavior had got even more unusual: if someone arrived unexpectedly at the flat, he'd curl up into a ball and rock; when we were out he'd bang his head against the sides of the stroller so hard that I had to cover the bars with soft blankets which he'd pull over his face to hide. I'd even started supermarket shopping at night because there were fewer people around then to upset him.

You don't know what lengths you'll go to, though, until you're tested. All I knew was that things had to be a very specific way for George to be anything close to happy, so I gave him what he needed, just as any mother would.

Otherwise his emotions were like a boiling kettle he couldn't control and I had to protect him from them or else he would hurt himself—biting his arm until he drew blood, pulling his hair until his scalp was raw. Even when George was a toddler, I still carried him a lot, because it took only a few seconds for him to hurt himself.

Some days it felt as though we were both drowning, and the moments I held on to were when I curled myself around George's small sleeping body after he'd finally fallen asleep and we lay together—the calm after the storm. It was the closest I got to touching him, and as I gently twisted a small curl of hair on his forehead, I'd look at George, so peaceful, and wish I could find a way to make him feel like that when he was awake. He seemed almost tormented by life, and that's any mother's worst fear, isn't it?

Now I watched as Lewis walked back into the room, trailing the long tube that still fed him oxygen from two prongs underneath his nose. They had slipped out of place and as Lewis sat down to play, George kneeled down and gently pushed them back into position. It was something he did with Lewis a lot and whenever I saw him do so, I knew there was love inside George.

"He's going to need a nappy change before we go," I said to Mum as I got up off the sofa.

I walked over to George and took a deep breath before picking him up, knowing I had a split second before his screams started. As I carried him to the changing mat I'd spread out on the floor, he started twisting and turning in my arms. Kicking and biting, he roared with rage as I laid him down with one arm across his chest and used my free hand to take off his nappy. George's face was bright red with anger, but I didn't look at him or try to make him laugh with words and smiles. It would only make things worse if I did, because George hated making eye contact with anyone. It was just one of the things I had had to learn: no one could comfort him with a kind look—not even me.

One year on the estate turned into two and I carried on studying for the Knowledge. Now don't go thinking because it took so long that I'm daft. I might not have been top of the class at school, but most people need at least a couple of years to pass the Knowledge and I was no different. Dad had managed to borrow for me an old cab to practice in, instead of going out on a moped as most people do, so a couple of times a week I'd go out and drive the runs, trying to drum the routes into my head.

All that practice had to be tested, and for that I had to make what's known as appearances at the public carriage office in Penton Street, north London. Think of it as what White Hart Lane is to Tottenham fans—the place where everything really important happens. Licensed drivers go there to have their cabs checked or for paperwork to be done, while trainee ones go there to be tested on their runs.

You could have cut the tension in the air with a knife as we all waited in a gray room to be called in one by one by two middle-aged men in suits, who asked us to recite runs before grading us on them from A to D. It's known as calling over a run, and you always knew how well you were doing by the marks you got and how quickly you were called back for another appearance. If it was 14 days you were getting better; if it was more than a couple of months you still had a long way to go. The worst bit, though, was that there was no definite end to it all, no set list of grades you had to get to pass the Knowledge. Instead, you just got called back again and again until one of the men in suits decided you were ready. It was like running a marathon with no idea of where the finishing line was.

I went up to London about every month to be tested and it terrified me. If the men in suits had shone a light in my face and told me I had to sleep on a bed of nails, I wouldn't have been surprised. They really knew how to lay down the law and they wanted to see a good attitude, nice manners and confidence: if you hesitated or got in a muddle as you called over a run, they'd give you a D grade without blinking; if someone's tie wasn't straight, they'd tell them to come back another day; and one bloke who swore in the middle of being tested got sent away in disgrace. We were all scared stiff of them, and you could hear a pin drop whenever one of the testers walked into the room where we all had to wait. Some women drive London cabs but not many, and I didn't meet any when I was studying. It was a world full of men, and those in suits stared at my curly hair, which always had that just-stuck-my-fingers-in-a-socket look however much I brushed it. Sometimes I wanted to scream when they looked at me like that. What did they know? I had George at home, I'd hardly slept and I was doing the best I could. But they didn't want to hear excuses.

Dad encouraged me every step of the way, though.

"Have you been out to practice, Ju?" he'd ask when I went round for a cuppa. "Are you going up the carriage office soon?"

I tried the best I could, but after more than two years of studying I had almost had enough of the whole thing. By April 1999 my grades had gotten better and I was being called back more quickly for appearances, but I was so exhausted by trying to study and coping with George that I just wanted to give up. The other thing that was putting me off was Dad's illness, because he was so bad by now that he was in and out of hospital. All I really wanted to do was be with him, not staring at road maps and trying to get somewhere I was beginning to think I'd never reach. So one day when I was due at the carriage office for an appearance, I went to visit Dad in the hospital instead.

"What are you doing here?" he asked as he lay on the bed. "Aren't you supposed to be in Penton Street?"

"I can't face it today, Dad. I'd rather just see you. I'll go another time."

"What are you on about?"

"I'm not going in."

It was as if a bomb had gone off under him.

"You're having a bloody laugh, aren't you, Ju?" Dad cried as he started struggling to sit up, wriggling around as he tried to get out of bed. "Get me up! Get me stuff! Get me tobacco tin! Don't forget me matches."

"But you're not allowed to leave the hospital, Dad."

"Well, I am if that's what it takes to get you to that appearance."

"Don't be stupid, Dad. You're in no fit state to go anywhere."

The farthest he ever went was downstairs to have a cigarette, and even then I had to push him in a wheelchair. He was never going to make it 10 miles into central London.

"Don't you go telling me what to do, my girl!" Dad cried. "We're going into town."

There was no arguing with Dad when he got an idea into his head. He wasn't even supposed to leave the hospital, but he had decided he was going to. We didn't quite have to dig our way out like they did in *The Great Escape*, but I still felt like a prisoner on the run as Dad told me to get him into his wheelchair, out to the car park and into the passenger seat of my car. We both knew the nurses would go mad if they knew what we were up to.

"I've got a good feeling about today, I have," Dad kept saying when we finally left. "You're going to do it, Ju. I'm sure of it. They're going to pass you today."

But no matter what Dad said, I was still panicking by the time we got into central London. I hadn't prepared myself for an appearance and didn't know if I could face it. I felt flustered and worried sick as Dad lay beside me in the front seat, which I'd had to push all the way back because it was too painful for him to sit up.

"I don't know where I'm going," I wailed as I drove toward a massive roundabout.

"Hold on!" Dad said. He lifted his head just enough to see over the dashboard and knew instantly where we were. "Over to the right, Ju."

I tried to pull across.

"Right, RIIIGHT," Dad shouted.

I pulled the car across three lanes of traffic and prayed for the best.

"Left," Dad said with a puff of exertion and pain.

We made it to the carriage office, but I was in a daze by the time I walked in for my appearance. I must have reeled off my runs like a robot, because the man in a suit looked a bit dazed himself when I'd finally finished.

I looked up at him and waited to find out when he'd want to see me next.

"That's it," he said. "You're out."

I stared at him. I'd done it? I'd got the Knowledge?

I could hardly believe it was all finally over as I walked outside to the car. I'd left Dad in his seat, but as I got into the car I saw a livid red burn mark on his chest. He'd dropped his cigarette while I was away and hadn't been able to pick it up with his crippled hands. He'd had to lie all alone while it burned a hole in him.

"Oh, Dad!" I said, as tears rushed into my eyes.

"All right, Ju?" he replied and smiled.

"Your chest, Dad. Are you OK?"

"Don't worry about it, love. It don't hurt."

"Are you sure?"

"Yes. Forget that and tell me how you got on."

As I looked at him lying there, I felt so full of love for him. "I did it, Dad, I did it."

A huge smile stretched over his face. "I knew you would," he said.

With a sigh, Dad leaned his head down against the seat. "Now let's get back to the hospital. Those nurses are gonna have my guts for garters."

Chapter 3

Now I wish this was one of those really happy stories where I became a taxi driver, gave a lift to a movie star and ran away with him into the sunset. But real life's not usually like that, is it? At least mine's not, and what actually happened two months after passing the Knowledge was that my life changed in a way that made me think I'd never be happy again.

George was the only thing that got me out of bed when Dad died, because losing him felt like the end of the world. We gave Dad the send-off he deserved—his coffin lying in a glass-sided carriage drawn by a horse wearing black feather plumes and led by a man wearing a top hat and tails, with friends and family following behind in a long line of taxis—but it felt unreal. How do you say goodbye to the person who ties you to the earth and stops you flying away with his jokes, kind words and quiet love? It wasn't just me who was lost—Mum and Dad had been together since they were teenagers. We all dealt with his death the best way we knew how: by staying close as we started learning how to cope without him.

Dad was buried in the local cemetery and I hated leaving him there, cold in the ground, so I visited him as often as I could and would sit with him as George and Lewis ran around together.

"Can we fill in the hole, Ju?" Lewis asked me one day when they found a fresh pile of dirt beside a newly dug grave that was waiting to be filled.

"Just a bit," I said.

A few handfuls of earth wouldn't matter, I thought to myself as I watched Lewis laughing while he played. He wheezed at the same time because laughing took all his breath, and he sounded like an 80-year-old man who'd smoked a pack a day all his life. George silently watched Lewis as he roared, as if he was trying to work out what the strange sound was. Then when Lewis started coughing with the effort of laughing, George bent him over before patting him on the back until he got his breath back. Sometime later I knew George would suddenly stop playing, stand to attention in the silence like a rabbit hearing a fox and listen to the sound of a train that no one else could yet hear until it rumbled past on the railway line running beside the cemetery. George was so sensitive to noise that when we were out for a walk he'd scream each time a car went by, as if a juggernaut was rushing by instead of a Ford Fiesta.

A few months passed like that—George and I going up to the cemetery, sometimes with Lewis, sometimes just the two of us, while I sat and wondered what the future held for us now that my dream of being a taxi driver had come to nothing. After doing the Knowledge, I'd just needed to pass a driving test in central London to get my full license, but I'd failed twice while Dad was still alive and I could not face taking it again after he died. He'd always encouraged me to keep going, but I could hear him laughing and see his face every time I got into a cab. It was too much, so I'd given up on all that hard work. I felt like a complete failure. I was no good as a mum and now I was a quitter too.

So time went on, as it does, the earth settled on Dad's grave and when a huge dip appeared, I almost got arrested after deciding to lay some turf on it as the sun went down one day. Within a few minutes, a couple of cops had arrived—black helmets on their heads and radios crackling—and it had taken some convincing to make them realize that I wasn't up to no good. But apart from being suspected of grave robbing, I liked going to the cemetery because it was somewhere peaceful to think.

However much I did, though, I still felt as if I was stuck in treacle. As George played, the thoughts would tumble through my head. The life I was giving George was a world away from the one that Dad and Mum had given Boy, Nob, Tor and me as children. And no matter what I did, I couldn't seem to find a way to make things better. I had been taught to earn my way in life and even had with my own small florist's shop, where I'd worked seven days a week before George was born, but I'd given it up when I became a mum. Now that the Knowledge had come to nothing, I didn't know what to do. It all made me feel so useless and as the months passed without Dad, I'd sit and wonder whether I was ever going to be able to change things for George and me.

But the more I thought about it, the more I knew one thing: I couldn't let my unhappiness get the better of me. It was time for a fresh start.

George was four when he began school in September 2000 and it was one of those days when I looked at him and wondered what I was making such a fuss about. With his big blue eyes and blond hair, he looked perfect as I dressed him in a bright red sweatshirt and black trousers. I felt sure that school was just what he needed now that we'd moved on to a new estate, which seemed so much nicer than our last. It was a new beginning for both of us.

As I say, I'm a dreamer. It took only a few weeks for me to be called in to talk to the teachers.

"We think George might have hearing problems," one said.

"He doesn't respond when we call his name," another told me.

"He can't seem to understand commands," someone else piped up. "If we tell the children we're going to sit down in a few minutes George does it immediately, and when we get them into a circle for story time, he crawls backward and lies under a bench with his hands over his ears."

In a way I was almost relieved to hear what the teachers had to say, because they were the first professionals to spend any proper time with George and they could see there was a problem, which was what I'd been trying to tell people for years. But I also felt scared, because however much you can cope with things when they're hidden at the back of the cupboard, they feel much bigger the moment they're brought out into the light. As George was referred for sight and hearing tests at a local clinic, I told myself that I could not be fearful: I was 27 years old, a grown-up, and if he really did have problems, the sooner they were identified, the sooner they could be sorted out.

Meanwhile, I kept to myself on the new estate after all that had happened on the old one and the first thing that needed sorting out was our new home, because the old woman who'd had the flat before us had lived there with 13 cats and the place was crawling with fleas. While the council came in and sprayed the rooms, George and I had stayed with Mum, and then it was all hands on deck when we finally moved in. I might have thought I was Miss Independent, but I still needed my family to help decorate.

I'd learned young, after all, that you have to make the most of your home. "Sides, top, then front," my nan Doris would tell me as she pointed at a wardrobe before handing me a massive bottle of polish and a duster when she got me over to her house every Saturday morning to help her clean. Usually I did a good job, but then came the day when I was about 10 and she suddenly hit me across the back of the head without a word of warning.

"Stay still!" Nan screamed as I saw stars. "Don't move. I'm going to get your mother."

She ran next door, came back with Mum and together they peered at my head.

"Look at them," said Nan.

"It's those kids from down the road who gave them to her," said Mum.

"What's wrong?" I asked.

"You've got head lice," Mum told me and I started to cry.

I was back to normal after a good shampoo with the nit lotion and Nan let me back in her house to help clean it again. But all those years of dusting had taught me the power of elbow grease, and that was what I used in our new flat. Soon the kitchen was painted terra-cotta, the hallway white, my bedroom pink and George's room yellow. I didn't just decorate the inside, though. Our third-floor flat had a balcony overlooking a field with a willow tree in it, so I made the most of the view by covering the balcony floor in rainbow stripes, painting the walls green and putting flowers in pots. Standing on the balcony blowing bubbles at George, because he could never get enough of them, I'd look at the shed roofs below and wonder if a bit of turf would make them look better. You can't even grow grass on a roof, but I never know when to stop, do I?

Real life came back with a bang, though, whenever I left the flat with George, because some days getting him to school could take up to an hour. He'd bite me or cling on to railings as we walked, screech and shout, or stare at the soldiers standing at the gates of the local army barracks and refuse to be moved. It was such a battle that I often took him in a stroller, and as I bumped it down the stairs, I began meeting the woman who lived in the flat below ours. I wasn't quite sure what she made of me, because our walls were paper thin and George made a lot of noise, while the only thing I knew about her was that she loved vacuuming so much that she seemed to be at it all day, every day.

The woman looked about the same age as me and had two children: a little boy around four, like George, and a girl who was a bit older. Even though we smiled as we passed on the stairs and she looked normal enough, I didn't stop to chat because I'd just moved from a place where a lot of people were either falling down drunk or stealing from washing lines, however innocent they looked.

But one day, the woman looked at me as I struggled up a step with George.

"Disgusting, isn't it?" she said as she looked at the gray concrete walls of the stairway.

They were covered in graffiti and the smell of wee wafted up from the corridor below because people were always peeing in it.

"Horrible," I said.

"I'm Michelle," the woman replied with a smile.

"I'm Julia."

"Good to meet you. Now, shall we get something done about these stairs?"

That was the start of our friendship. Michelle and I were united in stair rage as we got everyone together and went to see the housing manager.

"People will only have pride in their homes if you give them a reason to by cleaning up the graffiti and getting rid of the dog mess," we told him.

The housing manager agreed that if Michelle and I jetwashed the stairs and corridors, the council would paint the walls, and we were asked to pick a color. So what did we choose? Cream, maybe? White? Blue even? No: pink, pale, baby pink, because it looked lovely with the gray concrete floor, didn't it? We got so stair proud in the end that we even stuck fake flowers on the walls and would stand on our balconies watching troublemakers walk into the building. "Hope you're not going to let the dog pee in there," we'd shout to one man, who we knew let his pet loose in our corridor. He didn't like that one bit, but Michelle and I did. We'd been bitten by the brightening-up bug and even ended up painting the doors of the storage lockers each flat had on the ground floor to make the place a bit more colorful.

But however much Michelle and I got on, I was still backward in coming forward about being proper friends. Once I might have longed for a friend of my age, someone to see a film with or do a bit of shopping with maybe. But I'd learned that I was the only person who could keep George calm and because of that it wasn't fair for him or anyone else to leave him. His needs had to come first and I just didn't want to go out without him.

So while there were bad days when I cried quietly after he'd finally gone to sleep, I soon picked myself back up again and got on with things. I was George's mum and I'd got used to keeping both of us out of the way of most people. We saw family, of course, but I didn't want George to be stared at by strangers when he lay on the floor stiff as he had a tantrum or hear a tut as he screamed the place down. I didn't want to have to explain how I was getting called into school because he got into trouble with the other kids, hitting or biting them when they didn't play how he wanted, or how I'd asked for his hearing and sight tests to be done again because although they'd come back normal, now that George was at school I was more certain than ever that something was wrong. I might have gotten used to his ways when it was just the two of us, but I couldn't ignore how different they were now, which is why I wanted the tests to be done again in case there had been a mistake.

How could I explain all that to Michelle, whose children, Ricky and Ashley, were perfect? Tell her that George had begun to blurt out things when we were out and just wouldn't stop, no matter how many times I tried telling him?

"Fat!" he'd say as a larger woman walked past.

"Hairy!" he'd cry at another with a plait.

"Moles!" he'd shout at someone with freckles.

"Smelly!" he'd tell just about anyone if they got too close.

People looked at him strangely before carrying on their way, but however much I tried telling George not to do it, he couldn't keep quiet. The school didn't know what to make of him and had even started keeping a book in which they listed all his behaviors, like refusing to drink in front of people or disappearing for half an hour when he went to the loo because he took off all his clothes before going. There were so many little things that I did not know where to start, and that's why I was scared of making a friend.

Luckily nothing seemed to worry Michelle as we started to spend more time together. Maybe it was because she was a trained child minder, or just that she was really patient, but Michelle took everything in her stride—even the day when we were out on the field and I looked across to see George had pinned Ricky to the ground and was hitting him.

"Stop!" I screamed as I ran toward them.

George didn't turn around at the sound of my voice and when I finally reached him, he just looked at me blankly for a moment before hitting Ricky again.

"George, no!" I said as I pulled him off, thinking that this time he'd really done it and Michelle would never speak to me again.

But she was quietly fine about it. "These things happen with kids," she told me as I dragged George away.

It made me so sad to realize that he could not make friends. As I watched him with Ricky and Ashley, I could see that George didn't understand how to be with other children. I still wasn't brave enough to talk to Michelle about it all, though, until she brought it up one evening as we sat on the stairs between our flats. We'd gotten into the habit of meeting there as time had gone on and I'd found myself looking forward to the moment when I heard Michelle's knock. Leaving our front doors ajar so we were both near enough to hear if any of the kids woke up, we'd sit out together, and that's where we were the night she turned to me.

"Is there a problem with George?" Michelle asked.

No one had ever said it straight out like that before.

"I think so," I said. "But he's had his hearing and sight tested and they say he's fine. I'm at the end of my tether with it, though, because I'm sure there's a problem and no one seems to want to listen."

Michelle looked at me with her big eyes. "You know, you've got to stop apologizing for him, Ju. George is who he is and people are going to have to accept that. You get into too much of a state about it all. You shouldn't care so much about what other people think. I can see how much it bothers you, but it shouldn't."

"What about when he hits Ricky, though, or tells Ashley that she smells?" I asked. "What am I supposed to do then?"

"You do as much as you can with him. I know that. But

sometimes you have to let the kids sort it out themselves and know that people are going to have to accept George the way he is because he's not going to change anytime soon."

I've always thought we meet people for a reason and Michelle was my karma. As we got to know each other better, I'd talk to her about George: how I'd finally get him to sleep each night just hoping we'd get through a few hours without him getting up to wee up the wall or how I'd see other kids playing together and wish George could learn to join in.

"Let him be, Ju," Michelle would tell me. "You can't make George be what he isn't, and anyone can see what a good mum you are. It's other people who've got to change their attitude, not George. If they can't accept him, then they're not worth bothering about."

Michelle was so understanding that I soon even felt comfortable enough to take George to her flat. It didn't matter if he wiped cake up the wall there or bashed the head of Ashley's doll against the wall, because Michelle didn't flinch.

"Are you knocking some sense into Barbie, then, George?" she'd say with a laugh. "That's good."

And while George still found it hard to get on with Ricky and Ashley, even though they were both really good with him, I knew that he liked Michelle. He'd never hug her, of course, or smile—George wouldn't even look at Michelle when he spoke to her most of the time or show that he noticed when she was there. But as the months passed, he started doing something that told me he did: he sniffed. Each day when we left the flat, George would take in a deep breath of fresh air and tell me that he could smell Michelle. Because even though her flat was one floor below us, he knew when she had a wash on and to George that smell meant Michelle. Somehow she had got through to him and George showed me in his own particular way that she had.

Chapter 4

I stopped still as I walked into the bedroom and saw George. I wanted to scream, but knew I had to be silent. Somehow he had opened the latch that locked the window and climbed outside. He was standing on the other side of the glass with his bare feet on the ledge next to the open window. We were on the third floor. I couldn't move too quickly or else I'd frighten him.

"What are you up to, George?" I asked.

He stared silently at a spot just past my head, his hands holding on to the frame.

Slowly I reached into my pocket for my phone and dialed 999. "I need help," I told the operator.

A voice on the other end took my details and my eyes didn't leave George as I put down the phone, praying that someone would get here soon. If he moved an inch he would fall. I should have known he might do something like this. George had no sense of danger at the best of times and didn't seem to feel pain either. If he fell over, he never ran to me or cried; he just got up and walked away, with his knee pouring blood if he had cut it. But lately he'd been jumping up and down a lot when we went for a walk and telling me he was flying.

"Are you, my love?"

"Yes."

"Where?"

"Over a big building."

"Really? Where else?"

"A tree."

I'd told myself George had a wild imagination and I was happy that he could dream. But now as my heart hammered and George looked at me I knew I should have kept a closer eye on him. I wanted to scream—knowing I had to stand still, longing to run at him—for what felt like forever, but was probably just a couple of minutes, until I heard the sound of sirens. I had asked the firemen to be ready to catch George if he fell because I couldn't let them into the flat. If he saw strangers I was sure he'd let go of the window frame. He just didn't understand that if he did that, he would fall. George thought he could fly like the birds.

I took a step forward, ready to rush at him and grab him if he let go with his hands. Then I looked at my watch as if it was any other day and I didn't have a care in the world.

"We're late, George," I told him. "We've got to get to Nannie's because Lewis is waiting to see us."

George looked at me, as if he was thinking about whether he wanted to move or not.

"They'll be wondering where we are," I said, trying to keep the panic out of my voice.

Inch by inch, George started shuffling back along the windowsill and my heart was in my mouth with every move he made. But the moment he put a foot through the open window, I gripped it so hard there was no way he'd be able to rock back and I pulled him down into the room with me.

"Good boy," I said, longing to cuddle him, knowing I couldn't. "But you know you mustn't do that again, don't you, George?"

He brushed himself with his hands where I'd touched him and looked at me without a shadow of understanding in his eyes. My hands shook as I followed George out of the room and even though I knew that from now on I would lock every window and door in the flat and hide all the keys, I was still at my wits' end as I talked it over with Michelle that night.

"We've got to show him, Ju," she said. "George can't see it himself, so we've got to show him what could happen."

The following morning Michelle arrived at the flat armed with a box of eggs, and we took George to the bedroom, where we opened the window.

"Do you see this egg, George?" Michelle asked as she held it in front of his face. "It's you, it is."

She dropped the egg out the window and George watched as it flew down and smashed on the concrete below.

"Now you try," Michelle said as she handed him an egg.

After throwing half a dozen out the window, we ran downstairs to find the concrete outside the flats covered in bits of yolk and shell.

George looked around with a blank face.

"You'll get broken too if you fall—just like you'll get broken if you step in front of a car," I told him, kneeling down to face him. "You're like an egg, George—you're fragile. Do you see?"

He didn't look at me or say a word, but at least we'd tried, and I was learning by now that if you said things enough to George they eventually went in. If most mums had to tell their kids a hundred times, I had to repeat it a thousand to George. How else was he going to learn to fit into a world he didn't understand?

His problems at school were only getting worse and I knew a lot of people thought George was just a naughty child who couldn't be controlled: he'd climb the fence as the teachers told him to get down, hide under the dinner lady's sari or push children over. He had to learn, so I'd try to talk to him every time I was called into school, but George just couldn't see that what he was doing was wrong. He didn't know the difference between a tap and a grab so rough it ripped another child's jumper, or even understand how to move around other adults or kids: every time we left school, he'd run through the gates crashing into people, leaving them staring at him. I'd tried everything I could to make him walk with me, but he always bolted the moment he got out the school door and as I chased after him, he would roll on the floor screaming the moment I touched him.

George just could not see that he was the one who was different, and every time I tried to talk to him about what he'd done wrong, he would tell me that he hadn't. What I was trying to teach him just didn't make sense and he was sure it was the other children who were the problem. But although I knew that I had to keep trying to help him understand the way the world worked, it felt more and more as if his school was almost giving up on helping me to teach him that.

In the December of George's second year at school, when he was about five and a half, I was told he couldn't join in the Christmas concert because it might spoil things if he had one of his outbursts. I knew George wouldn't notice if he wasn't at the concert, but I would because that's what mums do, isn't it?

Teachers don't spend twenty-four hours with children, though. They didn't know George as I did and see all the tiny details of his behavior—the good bits that were mixed in with the not-so-good ones. For instance, he might not seem interested in most of his lessons, but the one that always made George listen was history. So I'd started taking him to all the places I could think of—Hampton Court Palace and the Tower of London, Windsor Castle and old aristocratic houses—to give him the kind of days out that I'd had as a child when Dad and Mum had told us all about London's old buildings and I'd learned to love those kinds of places. My favorite had always been Hampton Court Palace; whenever I walked into the huge hallway with its marble stairs, old paintings and enormous chandelier, I'd imagine that it was my house.

It wasn't easy, of course. George didn't like all the people and I had to work out what he could and couldn't cope with. Going on the Tube was just too frightening, but we just about managed if we went in the car and I let him hide when the place we were visiting got too busy. George never talked about what we saw but I knew his favorite place was Windsor Castle because his eyes would open in wonder when we went in winter and the castle walls shone as the huge lights were turned on at dusk. Water, shiny things and lights were his true obsessions.

So although George wasn't getting on at school, I knew he was intelligent. He showed that he picked up on everything that went on around him by the things he did. When Mum mentioned in front of him one day that my nan used to throw salt over her shoulder out of superstition, he started doing the same; and when something interested George, whether it was Windsor Castle, trees and birds or water and fishes, he couldn't get enough of it.

But all his teachers seemed to see was a little boy who wouldn't do as he was told and was disruptive, not interested in learning and sometimes aggressive. In a class of about 40 children, they just didn't have the time to spend on him and I was worried sick that George would never get any help. That's why I agreed to see two counselors when I was asked to go back to the clinic where George had had his hearing tests, because the second set had also come back normal and someone somewhere had obviously decided that George's problems were down to me.

For the first few sessions with the counselors, George came with me and would hide behind my chair as they talked.

"What do you do when George lies on the floor and won't get up, Julia?" the women asked, all soft voices and knowing looks.

What did they think I did? Drag him up by his hair?

"Do you tell him 'No' when he smashes a toy?" I was asked.

45

Did they think I was afraid to say a word when he bashed up Buzz Lightyear?

"Why do you think he doesn't eat with a spoon?"

"How is George's relationship with his father?"

"Do you have a boyfriend?"

There was one word for those women and it's this: patronizing. All they saw was a single mum with an out-of-control child, and it didn't matter what I said to try to tell them any different.

"Why don't you talk to the school?" I'd ask again and again. "They can tell you more about George and all his odd behaviors. This isn't about discipline. I know there's something more."

The answer was always the same. "George is still very young, Julia. This is an assessment and it takes time."

So I'd go into the school and ask them why they couldn't do something more for George.

"You're being assessed, Julia. It takes time."

I wanted to bang all their heads together, because the longer this went on the worse it was getting, and I felt even more frustrated when I was sent to a group for parents whose children had behavioral problems. It was the first time that I thought I might go to the top of the class because the advice was so basic.

When your child's been put in the box marked "naughty," it's hard to get anyone to see past it, and sometimes I wished the school could just let George be a bit. For instance, he was still very specific about what he would and wouldn't eat, and while he didn't tell me in words, I realized over time that he couldn't eat food that touched: he liked eggs, he liked baked beans, but if they were together on a plate he would just stare at them. It was as though George had the Berlin Wall of food inside his head because things always had to be divided. So I started giving him everything in separate bowls when I realized that it was the only way he'd eat.

He also had food phases—first it was just crackers, then squeezy yogurts and then custard creams—and I knew it wasn't just fussy eating because George got really anxious sometimes as he stared at his plate and breathed deeply. So I gave him what he wanted to calm him down enough to eat. It was during his jam sandwich phase that I wished the teachers might let him alone a bit. George's sandwiches had to be very particular because he wouldn't eat them if there was butter peeping out of the side of the bread; and even when I made them right, he often ended up chewing the sandwich before spitting it into his lunchbox. The teachers didn't like that at all, and although I explained that I'd seen a dietician who'd reassured me that George would be fine as long as he had milk, yogurt and bread each day and that I would sort out his lunchbox when he got home, they wouldn't listen. I felt drained by it all. Why did people keep asking questions? Why didn't they just do something to help?

Part of me said I had to keep trusting the doctors, who told me that George was still too young to be diagnosed with anything if there was something wrong with his development, the counselors, who told me to count to three, and the teachers, who kept saying that children learned at different speeds. Another part wanted to tell them all to just do something, anything, as one year at school turned into two and then three. After going on his first school trip,

I was told George couldn't go again because he wouldn't sit on his coach seat; when he went swimming—something Howard had taught him to do that he loved and was really good at—the teachers said he didn't listen and almost stopped him from going until I pleaded with them; and when I picked him up from school and was told he'd fallen asleep in class again because he'd hardly slept the night before, I'd see the questions in their eyes. George spent more and more time out of the class sitting in a long corridor at a small table with a teaching assistant by his side; it seemed as if it was a case of out of sight, out of mind.

I couldn't be sure, of course, but I wondered if George was picking up on it all, because while he'd always hidden away from people, he seemed to feel more and more that they were actually against him.

"He's watching me," George would say as we walked past a man on the way to school.

"No, he's not, love," I'd tell him. "He's just walking to work minding his own business."

Or George would pull down his Pokémon baseball cap and tell me the sun was watching him or the clouds were following us. Getting him to the dentist was so hard that I had to take him to hospital for an anesthetic when he needed teeth removed and he'd told me that the doctor had tried to kill him when he woke up.

I think that's why I tried to give him as much love as I could when we were at home, so that he'd at least feel safe with me when the world frightened him so much. But however much I gave him, George never expressed any love back, and even though I had a child, at times it almost felt as if I didn't. I'd find myself staring at other kids running out of school to give their mums a kiss and longing for George to want to hug me, but he never let me touch him or showed any emotion toward me. It was almost as if it was the first time he'd seen me when he woke up each morning and I struggled with it every day, sometimes even wishing I could meet someone and have another baby just to know how it felt to be a mother to a child who loved me back.

The only time George would let me touch him was when we rough played and he pretended to be a Power Ranger as we sat together in one of the tents I'd put up all over the flat because he liked them so much. I had even put one up on my bed, hoping he might sleep in it, because George could sit in a tent for hours on end. Most days I'd climb in with him for anything up to three hours at a time and that was when we'd play fight. As George climbed on to me, I would hold on to him for a few seconds as I felt the chubbiness in his legs or his skinny little chest. I loved those moments together because otherwise George didn't let me touch him. He did not really speak to me either: he still only talked about very specific things like Power Rangers and Buzz Lightyear. Often he spoke just single words or would chant phrases over and over again.

"Oh and the plane, oh and the plane," he'd cry a hundred times before moving on to something else.

I tried to distract him with puzzles or pots of paints but George would scream if he got anything wrong, which made it hard to play because everyone makes mistakes when they're six. One of the few things he liked, though, was play-dough, which he'd squidge in his hands as I made things for him to look at. So one day I bought him a plastic figure of a man with holes in his head to push the playdough through to make "hair." At first George smiled as he watched me do it but the moment I picked up some scissors to cut the hair, he started screaming. Throwing himself on the floor, he went stiff with rage as he roared. His shouts were so loud and sudden that I wondered if he'd somehow hurt himself and I knelt down beside him.

"George," I pleaded with him. "Tell me what's wrong."

But I never did find out because George didn't tell me how he felt. How could he? George didn't even seem to know who he was. When I'd stood him in front of a mirror one day, he'd cried so much that I'd had to take down all the others in the house. So how was he ever going to explain emotions that poured out of him in tantrums that still came out of the blue? George was like a mystery I couldn't solve, a puzzle whose pieces fitted together to make a picture I didn't quite understand, however much I wanted to.

Chapter 5

Did you know that a leaflet that drops through the door on an ordinary day can start something big? I didn't when one fell on to the mat about a year after I moved to the new estate. Ever since giving up the Knowledge and getting our new flat, I'd wanted to go back to work, because living off benefits made me feel a bit useless. So after George started school, I got a job in a pub, where I did the cleaning before going into the kitchens to help out the cook. I loved being out and about with people again, but slowly I realized that I couldn't keep working outside my home because I was exhausted most days after another night without sleep and I kept getting called into school about George. It took more than a year to accept that I needed all my energy to look after him, but in the end I had to give up work because he was such a full-time job. So that's why when the residents' association for the flats dropped a leaflet through our doors asking for mums to join I thought I'd give it a go, because I like to keep busy.

51

Now I can't say the association was the most exciting thing I'd ever done, because listening to someone from the council talk about where they're going to put speed humps just isn't that interesting. But something came out of it as I listened to people talk, because I found out that the piece of land beside the flats had once been a community garden. It got me thinking, because ever since moving into the flat and getting a balcony, I'd been growing things with George. He liked looking after plants and throwing mud around so much that our balcony was now full of pots of herbs, tomatoes, sunflowers and hanging baskets of flowers. His favorite thing was watering: George would fill everything to the brim, the flowers would struggle to stay alive and Michelle's balcony below would get covered in muddy water, which ruined her clean washing over and over.

So when I heard that the land by the flats had once been a garden for everyone to enjoy, I decided to see if we could bring it back to life. One of my neighbors, who'd lived on the estate for years, had pictures of how things once were and I wanted to try to make the land like that again. There were four blocks of flats on the estate with 50 families in each, so there should be enough of us to get something done. When I asked the residents' association for a grant, I told them that a gardening club might do a lot of good, because our estate had a bit of a past and maybe doing something that everyone could join in with might help. Things had changed over the years on the estate and ours, like many others, had become a real mix of nationalities. But the difference was that a few riffraff white people hadn't liked that and before I arrived an Asian family had been harassed. I didn't know for sure, but I thought that was why people had put up barriers to protect themselves from each other. Everyone kept to themselves and didn't encourage their kids to mix, which wasn't exactly good for community spirit.

Now some might say I'm simple, but we're not alive that long, so what's the point in fighting with each other? We've all got the same heart, whatever our differences, and while there were some bad types on the estate, most people weren't like that. There's always much more good than bad in any neighborhood and I was right about the gardening. When I got the grant from the residents' association people were ready to help. Dads came up to do the heavy work and clear the bit of grass next to the willow tree that we wanted to plant, while mums and kids helped Michelle and me with the planting.

After getting enough money to buy four benches, some equipment and a few rose bushes from the local pound shop, the gardening club soon became a weekly event. Old people arrived for a chat while children had a go with a trowel as I showed them how to dig in a plant and pack the soil down tightly around the roots to encourage them to grow or water the roses and take off the dead heads so that more buds would flower.

As time had passed with Michelle, Ricky and Ashley, George and I had started to go out a bit more with them. The kids would ride their bikes as Michelle and I chatted or we would go out to play on the green. So when George came with me to the gardening club, I was secretly hoping it might encourage him to mix a bit more. Although he stayed on the sidelines watching, I was glad if he just picked up a spade for a minute because it was a start and at least the gardening club was something for us to do together every week through the spring and summer. Most important, though, it sparked something inside Michelle and me, for we soon started thinking about what else we could do. Once we'd had stair rage; now we had community spirit fever.

So the next Easter, we decided to do an egg hunt for all the kids. I thought it was a great idea because one of my most fantastic childhood memories was a hunt I'd done as a kid. It was at my cousin Sally's house, which had a garden backing on to the River Thames, and Mum had put me in my best dress for it. It was magical to be there with all the posh boats going by as we hunted for eggs in the shrubs. My Aunt Rita was a very educated woman who'd done well in life and I remember thinking what a different life Sally led compared to mine. Even though I cried after finding so many eggs that Dad had told me to share them out, I never forgot that day, and those kinds of memories were what I had always tried to give George, because they're the ones that make you feel loved, aren't they? If some of the kids on my estate didn't have the best kind of life, maybe an egg hunt might give them a good memory.

Michelle and I didn't get any money for the Easter hunt from the residents association, but we saved up a bit to buy some chocolate and make posters letting everyone know about it. The hunt was fixed for midday, and so many kids turned up that as Michelle and I sent them off two by two I hoped there would be enough eggs for everyone. All sorts came: the good ones and the ones who were a bit naughtier. They all got as excited as each other—even Georgia, a girl with great big glasses and beautiful blonde hair who ended up jumping up and down underneath a tree turning the air blue with her swearing as she tried to get an egg down from the branches.

Community spirit can be in short supply these days, but I learned when Michelle and I did all those things on the estate that while you might not be able to change the adults who want to sit in their flats drinking and watching TV, you can encourage their kids out a bit more. In the years that followed, Michelle and I carried on doing things, and although she used to tell me that half the people thought we were stupid and the other half were sure we wanted something from them, I didn't care. That's just how I am and I think my mum and dad made me like that.

You have to break down the barriers if you can—just as we did after causing uproar when we decided to take down the washing lines outside the flats for a few hours one day to put up badminton nets for the kids instead.

"What are you up to now?" people cried when they saw what Michelle and I were doing. "Our whites need airing."

"Won't be long," we shouted.

Their smalls could wait a few hours. I'd played badminton as a kid and Dad had held my hand to help me. Now Michelle and I did the same as we got the kids to bat the shuttlecocks. As we played, I saw a little girl standing on one of the balconies. She was only about six and I could tell from looking at her that she'd been told not to come down, because she kept looking away when I tried to catch her eye. So the next time we played badminton, I knocked on the door of the flat where she lived and told her mum that I didn't have any certificates and I couldn't take her child all day but I hoped she'd let her girl come down. The mum didn't say a thing and I was a bit worried she might think I was a busybody. But she obviously didn't, because after that the little girl was sent down to play with us.

The best thing of all that Michelle and I did was start up a bats and balls night—although it got off to a rocky start. We'd got a bit cocky by then, what with the gardening and the badminton, so we decided that we wanted everyone to join in our bat and balls evening—even mums and dads. To spread the word, we used our secret weapon: the local gossips. You know the ones? Mouths like the Holland Tunnel and the time to stand around chatting for hours. I casually told them about what we were planning and knew they'd spread the word. But on the first night of our new club, Michelle and I took George, Ricky and Ashley down to the green and found just our friend Sharon waiting for us with her kids and a couple of old ladies. The gossips hadn't done quite as good a job as we'd hoped, but we had to carry on because people were watching from their balconies, staring at us and wondering what the nutters were up to now.

After that, we had to think of something else if our games night was going to work. We had to have a big plan. So Michelle and I decided that the best way to advertise the bats and balls was to have a family fun day on the green to let people know what we were about. After talking to my family, who agreed to help us out with money, we bought a cheap paddling pool and hired a bouncy castle for the day. We were so excited by it all that it was only as we stared at the paddling pool on the morning of the fun day that we realized it was going to take more than just a few buckets to fill it. The pool could have been used for Olympic laps.

"We'll have to use our kitchen taps," Michelle said.

So we hooked up hoses down to the pool, and that day turned out to be one of the best of my life. Loads of people arrived, and the kids jumped in and out of the paddling pool or on and off the bouncy castle, with Michelle keeping an eye on them all, while I started up a game of rounders to get people playing. George had come out and kicked his football as he watched lots of people play rounders. Even the man from the end of my block, who was so drunk he could hardly see straight to hit a ball, joined in.

"Now I know you like a drink, and I do too," I said, even though the most I ever had was a brandy and Coke and he must have had at least eight cans of beer inside him. "But I'm not sure you should have lager in your hand as we play games with the kids. It sets a bad example, doesn't it?"

The man looked at me, cross-eyed, before throwing his can up in the air with a smile. Later we talked and I found out his parents had died, and he'd become homeless and gone on the drink. Just shows that you can't judge what's on the outside, doesn't it? There's all sorts in this life, and I think the man had fun, even if he couldn't focus on the ball. We all had a good time that day, and the only bit of trouble came when the water tank on the roof burst because we'd left the taps running. As all the old biddies started moaning because they couldn't get a drop out of their taps, we had to phone the council to send someone out.

"What's been going on here?" the man asked as he stared at the massive paddling pool, loads of wet kids and sopping grass.

I had to tell him, but thankfully the man just laughed and went up on to the roof to fix things.

I always look back on that day with a smile. There were loads of us from all different flats, all different ages, who'd never really spoken to each other before, and the fun day broke the ice. After that more people started coming down to play bats and balls. It got so popular in the end that old people would come to sit on a bench and chat, and kids would be waiting for Michelle and me when we went to unlock the shed where we kept everything. I loved doing all that stuff and learned from it that behind every door there's a different story: the old woman I thought had lots of family was in fact lonely; an Asian family who'd always felt a bit unsafe on the estate were now comfortable enough to come out with their kids because they'd realized that most of us were friendly. Most of all I learned that when you do something for other people, you do something for yourself too, because as George and I got to know our community it felt as though we were beginning to have a place of our own. Maybe the world was opening up for both of us.

George's school was a real mix of kids. As well as all the ones who learned at an average pace, there were children who found it harder because they had special learning needs. By that I mean things like attention deficit disorder or physical disabilities that meant they needed more help than average kids. Some were taught in the special needs unit, while others had the help of a teaching assistant who sat with them for anything from a few hours a week to all day every day, giving them one-on-one attention during regular lessons.

Ever since seeing the counselors and doing the parenting course, I'd felt as if George was being forgotten by school, as I'd gone in and out almost as much as he had—either because he'd gotten into trouble again or to ask for something to be done—and it had felt as if I was bashing my head against a brick wall. Poor Mum had almost had her ear chewed off about it all as I talked to her about it over and over.

But something finally happened when George moved from the infants part of the school, where children spent their first three years, to the juniors, where he would be for another four until starting secondary school at 11. The school decided that from now on he was going to get some help from the special needs unit because he wasn't learning properly. Now that was more than a bit of an understatement: George was seven, couldn't read a word or write one, say the letter "A" if you held an apple up in front of him or recognize his own name when it was written down. I was glad something was happening because I can't tell you how it had all made me feel: some nights I'd lock myself in the bathroom and cry into a towel because I didn't want George to hear me upset. I felt lonely one day, sad the next, and then I'd try to be hopeful on the third.

As George started with the special needs unit, I was asked to go in to meet his teacher, Miss Proctor, who wanted to know all about his very specific behaviors, likes and dislikes. She didn't give much away as we chatted, but when I finally stopped talking, Miss Proctor looked at me with shock in her eyes.

"What on earth has George been doing since he started school?" she asked.

"I'm not sure," I replied.

"I know you're worried, and you are right to be, Miss Romp. George is very behind in class. He does not respond to anyone or show emotion to other children in a group. He also has outbursts which upset his classmates and he can be very violent at times."

For one awful moment, I wondered if Miss Proctor was yet another person who was going to decide that George was just a naughty child. Then I realized she wasn't: there are always two sides to every coin and instead of seeing him as a naughty and uncontrollable boy, Miss Proctor saw something different.

"It's been worrying me sick," I said in a rush, wondering if I was going to start crying on poor Miss Proctor, because it's amazing how emotional you can get after you've been coping for so long and someone suddenly says "That's a bit of a load, isn't it?"

"It's been hard ever since he was born and no one will listen," I told Miss Proctor. "George is almost like a stranger to me. I know that sounds awful, but it's how it feels, and I can't let him mix with most kids because I never know what he's going to do.

"He just doesn't seem at all interested in anyone—even me a lot of the time. There's no cuddling or laughter with George and all anyone has ever told me is that he'll grow out of it. It's hard because it's like he doesn't know who I am at times. I mean, he knows but it doesn't mean anything. It's like he doesn't really understand that I'm his mum."

Miss Proctor looked at me with her kind eyes. "We are going to help George," she said. "There are many techniques we can use and ways of getting children who've never been

interested in learning to start. George obviously has difficulties but there are ways around them."

I liked Miss Proctor from the moment I met her and was
glad she was going to oversee George as he moved between
lessons in the special needs unit and the regular classroom.
Don't get me wrong: it wasn't as though a magic wand had
suddenly been waved and the good fairy had come to rescue
us; Miss Proctor was working in a school with loads of kids.
But at least George was getting some help, and within a few
months an educational psychologist called Michael Schlesinger came into our lives. I was told he was going to assess
George to try to find out exactly what level his learning and
social skills were at, and I waited anxiously to find out what
he decided.

"I saw a man today," George said angrily when he came
home on the day I knew he'd seen Mr. Schlesinger.

"What kind of man?" I asked.

"He smelled of coffee."

"Really?"

"He sat close to me. He had big, stick-out eyes."

"Did he?"

"Yes. I don't want him to ever sit near me again."

I could tell George was worried but just hoped that Mr.
Schlesinger might be able to do something for him. For so
long, it had felt as if I was standing with George on a beach
after a shipwreck as people out at sea waved at us before
sailing by. Maybe now someone might try to rescue us just
a little bit.

A few days later I went to meet Mr. Schlesinger and
found a really tall man, well spoken and with kind eyes. I
immediately felt comfortable because he had a real air of

calm about him. Mr. Schlesinger started by telling me what he'd done to assess George—a range of tests like showing him picture cards and asking him what they showed.

"Brown," was the only word George had said after staring at a piano for several minutes.

Mr. Schlesinger told me that most children said music or singing when they saw the picture and that George had also had difficulty identifying facial expressions.

"He has severe learning difficulties and significant problems with social interaction," Mr. Schlesinger told me. "George's learning age is about that of a three-year-old. It's a very complex situation and we're only at the beginning of understanding it. But I can say that while George is going to need a lot of help, we are going to identify the problems and tackle them one by one."

I stared at Mr. Schlesinger silently.

"Are you all right, Miss Romp?"

I wasn't quite sure to be honest. After all those years and all that worry, a 24-carat expert had finally spelled out in black and white just how bad things were. But I didn't feel sad; I felt relieved. Mr. Schlesinger had seen past the blond, blue-eyed, perfect-looking boy that George was to the lonely, frightened child who was struggling inside him. I swear it was as if a ray of sunshine had peeped out from behind the clouds and I could almost feel it beating down on me.

PART TWO

Finding Ben

Chapter 6

Little did I know that a stray cat that looked as if it had gone 10 rounds with Mike Tyson when I first saw it would be the key to unlocking all the love and imagination that had lain trapped inside George for so long. Ben arrived in the summer of 2006, just after George had turned 10 and a few months after I'd finally been told that he had autism. During the two long years it had taken to get him diagnosed, after meeting Mr. Schlesinger, I'd thought that one of the many people who had got involved with us—from doctors and psychologists to teachers and a speech therapist—would hold the key to unlocking George. But life isn't logical, is it? While all those people had huge experience and put a lot of hard work into helping George, it was Ben who changed his life forever—and mine too.

Diagnosing George's problems had taken a long time because there were so many of them. First I was told he had ADHD (Attention Deficit Hyperactivity Disorder), which explained why he couldn't sit still in class or at home. But it didn't feel right when I was sent to a group for parents whose children had ADHD and watched as some of the mums and dads stayed silent while their kids smashed up the furniture. It was almost as though they were giving up on them, and that wasn't the way I wanted to deal with George. The pieces fell more into place when he started seeing a psychiatrist who assessed him for autism. She was the first person to talk to me about the condition and as she did, I realized it might be the key to understanding George's world. The doctor told me autism had a huge range of characteristics, which presented themselves in many different ways, and George was unusual because he had other problems as well, including ADHD and paranoid tendencies. The other thing that complicated the situation was that although George was quite talkative compared to some autistic children, he refused to speak to anyone who tried to assess him, so it was hard for them to work him out.

As the psychiatrist saw George week in, week out, she talked to me about what she had observed in him and everything she pinpointed—his sensitivity to smell and noise, his inability to make eye contact or bond with anything, his outbursts of temper and his obsession with rituals and routines—seemed to fit the diagnosis. The more the psychiatrist spoke to me about autism, the more sense it made. She told me that George's senses were much more powerful than the average person's, so the noise of a car sounded like a freight train to him, smells were overpowering and someone's touch felt threatening rather than comforting. As I listened, I began to understand so many things better—why George wouldn't let me near him, why he stared through me and even seemed to think at times that I was his enemy; and I was glad to finally see into his world, because I found it as hard as ever that George still didn't seem to know I was his mum, the person who loved him no matter what.

On a morning like any other, we had been rushing to get to school because George hadn't gone to sleep until 5:00 a.m., so he hadn't wanted to get up. Then his dressing routine had gone wrong because his T-shirt wasn't soft enough, so we'd had to take everything off and start again; and breakfast had been held up because I'd overcooked the toast, and then George had told me the crusts were too brown on the next loaf I opened (sometimes it was as many as four loaves before George decided on one he could eat), and I'd slapped butter on the toast so quickly that I'd dropped the knife on the floor as I put it down.

"I'll sort it out when I get home," I said as I gave him his breakfast.

A few hours after I got home from taking him to school, the phone rang.

"Miss Romp?" a voice said on the other end.

"Yes."

"I work for Hounslow social services. I wanted to speak to you because your son has made an allegation that we are investigating."

"What do you mean?"

"George has said that you stabbed him."

"Is this a joke? George hasn't been stabbed. I've just dropped him off at school."

"Well, I'm afraid he's told a teacher that he was stabbed in the side with a knife."

"Are you serious?"

"Yes, Miss Romp."

I could hardly believe what I was hearing. Of course there was a big investigation. I was interviewed, George was interviewed and it all went on until everyone realized that I hadn't attacked him. But somehow that knife falling on the floor had made George think I'd tried to hurt him and the way he looked at me for days afterward turned me cold. It was as if he was made of glass and couldn't see me. He stared straight through me and wouldn't say a word.

"My mum tried to kill me," he said again and again. "My mum tried to kill me."

Can you imagine hearing those words from your own child? But the psychiatrist helped me to understand them, by telling me that George's autism meant that everyday things, even a knife dropping on a floor, could seem threatening.

At first the word "autism" scared me, because I didn't properly understand it. But after the doctor had patiently answered all my questions, I'd go home with the notes I'd written to look things up on the computer and began to see into his world more.

Don't go thinking life was perfect now that the professionals were involved. We didn't always see eye to eye and it's hard to disagree with people who've got degrees and certificates. For instance, the psychiatrist told me that George's ADHD might improve if he was given medication, so I agreed to let him have it. But I stopped the pills after watching George lie on the sofa with dribble coming out of his mouth and a dazed look in his eyes. I didn't need textbooks or a white coat to know it wasn't right.

"I'd rather deal with him just like I always have than see him like this," I told his doctor.

Part of me was scared that after all the years of asking for help, we might not get any more because I hadn't taken the advice I'd been given. But I had to do what I thought was right. Drugs might be tested and people might have been trained for years to hand them out, but while pills were obviously the best thing for some children, they weren't for George.

But although his psychiatrist and I had a difference of opinion about that, she was very good to me otherwise; and while a diagnosis didn't suddenly make things right, they felt a bit easier because at least I knew what I was dealing with now, and that meant I could learn to help George cope with the world a bit better. The only thing I found really hard, though, was when the psychiatrist told me that George would probably never learn to show his love for me in the way most kids do with their mums.

"This is a condition he will live with for the rest of his life," she said. "You can improve your life by understanding autism and learn how George works, but autism is never cured. George is never going to be the cuddly boy you wish for, Miss Romp. It's all part of his condition and there's no magic cure."

That was the thing that almost did it for me. Forget the behavioral problems, the food issues, the tantrums and mood swings. The fact that George didn't seem to need anyone or anything, even me, was what I'd always struggled with most and I'd fought against it all his life. I'd tried to give him what I'd had as a child in the hope that he'd one day find some happiness in the family and friends around him. But maybe I'd been stupid to hope for so long, because the doctor seemed to think it would never happen.

So what did I do? Give up? Get realistic and accept George would never show me his love? No. Never. I told myself that the doctor was a doctor and I was his mum. I would carry on trying while there was still breath inside me to show George that he could be part of the world and help him find his place in it. It was the worst thing in the world to watch George struggle each day with his frustration and anger, and while I had learned to accept that he was different and love him for who he was long before he had been diagnosed with autism, I would not stop trying to help him improve now that his condition had been given a name.

Deep down I felt sure that somehow, somewhere, I would find the key to unlocking some of what was inside him and give him some peace, if not the happiness that I'd always wanted for him. But you could have given me a thousand years to find that key and I'd never have imagined it would come in the shape it did: a fluffy black and white cat with bright green eyes. So when I first saw it on a morning just like any other, I had no idea this cat was going to change our lives forever.

The cat looked thin and sickly as I stared at it, standing on the roof of the shed in the garden George and I had now that we'd moved. The year before the council had given us a lovely two-bedroom house close to Mum and Lewis, and it came with 16 feet of outside space that was more of a mud pit than a garden. But after putting down turf with a stepping stone path running through it, I planted roses, honeysuckle and clematis and tracked down a secondhand shed on the Internet that I stained pale green and painted with flowers on the inside; then I bought a mini summer-house in the same green. Every time I looked out and saw my lovely garden, I couldn't believe how lucky we were.

The first time I saw the cat in the distance, one morning in the summer of 2006, I could see immediately that it wasn't well. The cat was black and white, but it was so filthy that its white fur was stained brown and it disappeared almost as soon as I got a glimpse of it. I felt so sorry for it that I left out some milk and bread that night and the bowl was empty by the next morning. Over the next few days, I saw the cat again, but only ever for a few seconds because it would dart off the moment I opened the door to the garden. After a few days I managed to edge slowly across the lawn and get near enough to have a better look. I'd seen lots of feral cats before that lived in the wild and survived on whatever they could find, but this one seemed different. It looked really sick. It needed help.

As I got closer, the cat lifted its head. There was a bald patch running in a ring around its neck that was crusted with blood. It looked as though someone had almost tried to hang the cat, and its bottom was just as red raw. It also had a huge belly for such a scrawny thing and I realized with shock that it must be pregnant. In fact, it didn't look as if the cat had long to go until she had her babies. How was she ever going to be strong enough to have them?

I took a step closer to try to get a better look, and the cat panicked. Hissing and clawing at me, she jumped up on the fence and on to the shed roof, and streaked off. I wondered if I'd ever see her again now that I'd scared her, but cats are nothing if not greedy, aren't they? The stray returned for her bread and milk again that night and the next, and was soon visiting the garden during the day as well.

She seemed to like being there, but as I watched her come and go I felt more and more worried. I'd gone knocking on a few doors, hoping someone might have lost a cat, because it's not unusual for them to go off and not be able to find their way home; I'd also phoned the local animal charity to see if anyone had reported a black and white cat missing. She was very distinctive, after all. She had a patch of white fur shaped like a butterfly under her nose and a bib of white on her chest. Her eyes were also a striking green— pale but bright—the likes of which I'd never seen before. But no one was looking for a pregnant black and white cat. I knew I had to get her to the vet as soon as possible because her babies were going to arrive soon.

Now the reason I did all this was because I had become a bit of an accidental pet rescuer. It started when George and I were still living on the estate and Michelle had taken in a Labrador, which hadn't done well enough at training classes for its owner's liking. Michelle didn't have the space to swing a cat in her flat, let alone a bouncing puppy, but the dog was beautiful, all chocolate-brown fur and big eyes, so I could understand why she wanted to help. The only problem was that we weren't allowed animals, and there was no way Michelle was going to hide a half-grown Labrador when she started walking it on the estate and the gossips got moaning. "She got a dog in there?" I'd hear them say. "We're not having that! We've been in these flats sixty years, love, and there's no pets allowed. The council won't have it."

I told Michelle that the dog had to go or else she'd be reported. But instead of doing something sensible like giving it to a charity, we smuggled it up a whole floor to my flat, where pets were just as forbidden as they were in Michelle's. We didn't want to let the dog go until we were sure it had a good home, so we got it into my flat, where I tried to keep it as quiet as I could. Trouble was the puppy went berserk every time the doorbell went.

"Have you got a dog in there?" I'd hear someone say as I opened the door a crack.

"No, just the telly," I'd reply as the Hound of the Baskervilles howled two inches from me.

In the end, I had to say the dog was on holiday with me, although who'd want to holiday in Hounslow? It's not exactly Barbados, even for a Labrador. Fortunately after a few weeks, I found it a home with a man I knew in Kent and off it went to a lovely life by the sea.

So that's how my career as a pet rescuer had started and it carried on after we moved, thanks to George. He'd always liked animals and when Mum's dog Polly had died, he'd made a cross for her grave in the garden and told his nan that she could never move because that would mean leaving Polly behind. I'd explained to George that we weren't allowed pets in a council flat and taken him to city farms to see animals instead. He knew the pet ban would be lifted, though, when we moved into a house with a garden, and as soon as we did he started asking for everything from fish to birds to dogs. I got him a budgie—a bright yellow one that we called Polly—but she lasted only a few weeks because her singing was too much for George and she had to move in with Mum and Lewis. Then he decided he wanted a rabbit, but because Polly hadn't worked out that well I wasn't sure. So instead I took him to the local pet superstore to look at the rabbits, hoping that would be enough for him. Trouble was, we went in one day and I saw this big, beautiful, flop-eared bunny, George said he wanted it and I gave in. We called her Fluffy and she was soon installed in the flower-painted shed. But once again, George didn't stay interested for long and I told myself that he obviously wasn't going to bond with a pet, however much I wanted him to.

The neighbors knew we had a rabbit, though, because everyone knows everything on a housing estate—which is why a woman from round the corner knocked on my door after finding one hopping by the side of the road. She didn't know what to do with it, so I took it in and my unofficial animal foster home was open for business.

After that, things just snowballed. After taking in the rabbit and finding it a new owner by asking around, I had a stream of animal orphans in and out the house: the wild rabbit that a child had found in a local park, a white albino that went to a good home, and several guinea pigs that people had bought for their kids and ended up not wanting. I couldn't say no to any of them. It wasn't the animals' fault they were homeless, and I liked seeing the rabbits hopping around on the lawn, or shuffling, in the case of the guinea pigs—having a bit of fun at last.

But even though I'd loved animals ever since I was a child, I was determined not to be the official owner of anything other than a rabbit—and cats were top of the "not wanted" list. Mum had put me off them after she'd taken in so many stray cats when I was a child that I'd ended up being called "Hairy" at school because my uniform was always covered. I'd sworn to myself that I'd never have a houseful of animals. So when the rabbits and guinea pigs started arriving, I was happy to help but careful not to get too attached. I didn't give them names, because they were going to go on to proper, permanent homes. They were only ever called "guinea" or "rabbit." It was strictly business, or rather charity.

Then the stray arrived and everything changed when she started visiting our garden more and more. There was just something about her: the way she looked at me with her huge green eyes. She gazed at me like a wise old woman, so peacefully and reassuringly that even though she was determined not to let me touch her, I found myself looking forward to seeing how she was each day, wondering where she'd been and what she'd gotten up to, what kind of life she'd had that had brought her to my garden. I had to help her, and so I knew I had to catch her and get her to the vet. Soon I started leaving her food just inside the shed door next to a cat carrier, where I'd made up a nice comfy bed. Once she started sleeping in it, I'd close the door and take the cat to the vet.

She wasn't stupid, though. The cat soon started leaving hairs behind on the bed blankets, but she was never anywhere near the carrier when I went to see her and I'd go back in the house huffing and puffing with frustration.

"What's in the shed?" George asked me one day as I walked inside.

"Just a stray cat," I told him.

"Can I see it?"

"I'm not sure, George. She doesn't really like people. She's very scared, so I think it might frighten her if both of us go out there."

"Why's she here?"

"Because she's having kittens and I'm trying to help her."

That was it. George heard the word "kittens" and the next day when I went to see the cat there was nothing I could do to stop him from following me outside, because just like lots of other 10-year-olds, he was fascinated by the idea of baby animals.

"Stay well back," I told him. "She might claw at you if you get too close and I don't want you getting scratched."

George stood behind me as I opened the door and peered into the darkness. As I stared around, I couldn't see a thing in the gloom.

"There she is," George said, pointing.

I followed his finger and saw two green eyes shining out above our heads. The cat was sitting on a shelf looking down at us. And instead of running at it, George did just as I had told him and stood quietly beside me.

"She's going to have her babies soon, isn't she?" he said.

"Any day, I think."

After that he came out with me every day. But while George was always quiet around the cat, because he understood that I wanted to catch her, she was as determined as ever not to be helped. Each day we'd find her anywhere but in the carrier and she continued to hiss and claw if we ever took a step too close.

"What's wrong with her?" George would ask.

"I think she's scared."

"Why?"

"Because she's not used to people."

"Doesn't she know that we want to help her?"

"I don't think so."

I liked it that George wanted to help the cat as he looked at it sitting quietly in the darkness. As he'd always shown when he was with Lewis, George was drawn to anyone—or anything—that he thought needed his help. For George, the world was divided into two: the people who acted so strangely and had all the problems that he got blamed for and the ones who needed to be looked after.

"Boo!" George suddenly said to the cat and smiled.

The cat didn't move a muscle.

"Boo!" George said again and I stared at him in surprise.

George was trying to play. He wanted the cat to join in his favorite game of hide and seek—even though she wasn't having any of it. The cat stared at George, not batting an eyelid as he spoke, but the moment he took a step into the shed, she reared up like a vampire staring at a clove of garlic.

"Boo!" George exclaimed as he looked at her. "Baboo!"

"What's that?" I asked.

"Her name."

"Baboo?"

"Yes. Baboo."

The nickname stuck, and as days turned into weeks I woke up every morning convinced I'd find a litter of kittens and George stayed as interested as ever in the cat. But she still wouldn't come near us and I wondered how I was ever going to get her some proper attention. However much I fed Baboo, she was still very thin, apart from her big belly.

So one morning I decided enough was enough of the soft approach. After taking George to school, I walked into the garden and sneaked up to the shed door. Peering inside, I crossed my fingers because I needed a stroke of luck today.

I got it. The cat was asleep in the carrier and I carefully picked up a broom before pushing its long handle into the darkness. Holding my breath, I eased the carrier door closed and waited for the stray to explode in rage when she realized she'd been locked up in cat prison. But instead of hissing and spitting like a cartoon cat, she just sat quietly in the carrier as I closed the door. I could swear it was as if she was asking what had taken me so long.

Chapter 7

I tried telling myself the cat hadn't gotten to me when I dropped her off at the vet. But who was I kidding? I'd helped lots of animals before but this one was different. It was something about the cat's eyes and the way she looked at me, as though she was wise. I've always thought animals have souls, just as people do, and this one's soul seemed old; it was as if she wanted to tell me something she'd learned during all her years. But what?

After handing the cat over to the vet, I waited until he had examined her to find out how long it would be until she had her litter. The vet had other news, though.

"She's a he," he said when he'd had a look.

I stared at him. "What do you mean?"

"It's a boy."

"But what's that stomach if it isn't kittens?"

"A large cyst which needs to be removed. The cat has also been neutered, so he must have belonged to someone once."

The poor thing must have been abandoned or some-thing. As I left the vet, I told myself the cat was in good hands now; someone else was going to look after her, or rather him. Baboo was going to have an operation and then he'd be fine. It was time to go back to looking after my foster pets and keeping things simple. I had to forget the cat.

Only I couldn't, could I?

After leaving my telephone number so that I could get a progress report after the operation, I thought about the cat constantly. As I made up posters advertising a boy cat instead of a pregnant girl and told myself I was only doing what anyone would by helping to find its owners, I wondered how the stray was. After ringing the vet and being told the cat might not survive even after its operation because the cyst could have been a cancerous growth, I felt worried sick.

But even as I wondered if I could break my no-pets rule and George asked about the cat after every phone call to the vet, I couldn't bring myself to change my mind. How could I? I knew what would happen if I brought the cat home. It would be Polly and Fluffy all over again, and I had enough on my hands because looking after George was a full-time job. I was only 33 but felt like 100 some days because George still only slept for three or four hours each night. He was also getting more and more anxious as he got older, which had started to cause a whole new set of problems.

It had all begun the year before in July 2005, when London suffered a terrible day. Fifty-two people were killed when bombs went off on a bus and three Tube trains, and George heard all about it on the news. While once he'd quickly forgotten things that worried him, the bombings stuck in his head. He talked about them constantly, and as I listened I realized he believed that anyone with brown skin, like the men who'd carried out the London bombings, might be trying to hurt people. No matter how much I told him there was good and bad in all kinds—whether their skin was black, white or purple—he just couldn't accept it. The worst moment of the day was getting him on to a bus that was full of people going to work as I took him to school.

"There's a bomb on the bus, there's a bomb on the bus," George would chant if he saw anyone Asian carrying a rucksack.

Or he'd count down as he looked at them getting on. "Ten, nine, eight, seven, six, five . . ." he'd shout, as if waiting for an explosion.

It was absolutely terrible and I wished the ground could swallow us up when George did this. Knowing I wouldn't be able to make him stop talking, I'd put my hand over his mouth as people stared.

"Don't breathe on me, don't touch me," he'd shout. "I've got to get off the bus, stand back, don't touch me."

So I'd press the bell and we'd get off the bus a mile from school and have to walk the rest of the way.

One day the bus driver beat me to it, slamming on the brakes as George chanted. "You're going to have to get off," he called to me. "He's upsetting people."

I didn't know what to do. "He doesn't understand what he's saying," I told the driver. "He doesn't mean it. He's not a bad boy. It's because he's worried. He's not trying to upset people on purpose."

"I mean what I say. You've both got to get off. I can't

have this."

So as people tutted and stared, George stood up, oblivious to what was going on, and I got him off the bus. I could have cried as the doors slammed.

After that George's anxiety just got worse: he'd refuse to walk next to the criss-cross yellow lines of a box junction because he thought he'd fall into a hole and never get out; he'd gasp if my foot touched the lines between paving slabs and so we had to creep along to school without stepping on them; he'd stick his head in hedges when cars went by because the noise frightened him so much.

Just getting him into school was an ordeal, so how could I possibly look after a cat as well, even if I wanted to? I knew it wouldn't take much to care for one, but half the time I felt like a rubber band that was going to snap, and I couldn't take on a sick animal as well as everything else. George was still seeing his psychiatrist and although I knew he trusted her enough to go into her office and sit down while she talked to him, George was as distant with her as he was with everyone. As he played with toys and the doctor tried speaking to him, he'd stare out the window or tell her he didn't need to see anyone. He didn't like the therapy group he'd been sent to either and was still as much in his own world as he ever had been. So even if I did end up deciding that it would be good for him to have a cat, shouldn't he have a kitten that he could watch grow up, to give him the best chance of bonding with it, rather than an old cat that looked like something from an animal welfare poster?

Then the phone rang.

"The cat is ready to go home," the vet told me. "Do you

have one in mind?"

"I'm sorry but no," I replied.

I had to stay strong. Stick to my decision. I couldn't back down on this one.

"Well, would you think about visiting the cat?" the vet asked. "He seems sad. He's just sitting in his cage with his head hanging down. Maybe he'd like a visit?"

I was not going to take that cat home. I definitely wasn't.

But you already know what happened next: George walked into the room, the cat stared at him and George looked right back, gazing squarely into the cat's eyes. He never did that. He could not bear to meet anyone's gaze for more than a split second, and that was only with people like me, Mum and Lewis. Not strangers—and certainly not strange cats. Then George spoke to the cat in a high singsong voice I had never heard before. It was the kind of voice that people use for babies and small children, curling out of him, bright with affection, and the cat immediately listened. The stray who had not wanted us anywhere near him when he was living in our shed had a real change of heart when George spoke to him softly and sweetly, almost dancing to the rhythm of George's words as he rubbed up and down the bars of his cage and stared at George. They looked as pleased as punch to see each other. And the moment I saw the spark between them, all I knew was that my doubts were washed away. Baboo was coming home with us.

Baboo was like a basketball star, known by his nickname as well as by his official name. He was going to be called Ben as well as Baboo, because Mum had had a cat called the same years before and George wanted the name. I didn't care how many names the cat had because George was excited to have him home.

"When's he coming? When's he coming? When's he coming?" he asked in the days leading up to the one when we collected Ben from the vet.

I'd been told to keep Ben in a small, contained room for a couple of days: the vet had warned me that the first time I let him out of the small room, he would probably try to make a run for it. After making him a bed in a box filled with soft blankets, which I put in the downstairs bathroom, I kept a close eye on him. The most I could usually see when I opened the door to give Ben food or water was the tip of his nose peeping out from inside the box, because he was still very scared. Even when he did come out of his hiding place, Ben looked sorry for himself. What with a huge shaved patch and stitches where the cyst had been removed, and a cone-shaped plastic head collar to stop him nibbling them, he looked as though he'd really been through the wars.

George wasn't put off in the slightest, though, and kept going to check that Ben was still in the loo.

"He's in his camp," he'd say as he looked around the door and spoke in the high, soft voice that I had first heard at the vet's. "Are you OK, Baboo? Does he want his dinner? He does, he does, he does."

Whenever George spoke to Ben, he sounded like a Disney character. His high-pitched voice was soft and loving, a special voice just for Ben. I quickly realized that he was talking more as he told me where Ben was, what he was doing, whether he wanted a drink or food. Soon I started replying in the same kind of high voice to encourage him. Although I wasn't sure where our cat voices had come from or what they meant, I wanted to see where they might take us, because I had long ago realized that I would have to fit in with however George wanted to communicate. When he was about five, George had gone through a phase of barking all the time and I had worked out that two barks meant yes and one meant no. Cat talk might not last forever but while George felt comfortable using it I was going to join in, trying to bring the best out of every situation.

George obviously couldn't wait for the day when Ben was finally let out of the loo, but I wanted to give him a bit more time to get strong before we gave him his first taste of freedom.

"We're going to have to be really quiet when we let him out of the bathroom," I finally told George after Ben had been in there for a week. "He's going to be very scared, so we've got to keep still and not frighten him."

I pulled the loo door ajar and went into the living room, where George was sitting on a sofa. Nothing happened for a few seconds until Ben suddenly ran into the room. He was going like greased lightning—a streak of black and white fur heading straight for the window and freedom. His collar hit the glass before his body, sending him flying backward on to the floor. I thought I was going to faint as I watched Ben scrabble to his feet and dive behind the TV bench. After all the effort of catching him and getting him well, he'd probably done himself a terrible injury.

"Oh no!" George cried. "What's happened to him? We've lost him. Baboo has disappeared." Suddenly George started shrieking with laughter, laughter I'd never heard before, bubbling up out of him and erupting into the room like a volcano.

I seized the chance to play along. "Call an ambulance!" I said in my cat voice. "Ben needs a doctor."

"But he's hiding. He's frightened."

"Really?"

"Yes. He thinks the Power Rangers are going to get him."

"What are they going to do?"

"They're going to fight him. Ben's really scared."

"Well, why don't you talk to him? It might make him feel better."

George kneeled down on the floor. "Come out, Baboo. Come and see us."

George carried on talking softly in his cat voice, trying to get Ben to come out. Not only did he seem to understand that Ben was scared, we also had just had the kind of conversation that we did not usually have. When George was worried or upset he communicated very specifically through chanting or asking repeated questions. He didn't really have imaginative conversations like the one we'd just had, in which he used what I said to carry on talking.

"Baboo?" he called as he stared under the TV bench. "Is you scared?"

Ben wasn't going anywhere, though; all we could do was wait until he was good and ready to come out from his hiding place. But when he finally did, Ben walked into the middle of the room, looking as calm as I'd ever seen him. It was as if he had been wrestling with a big decision while he was hiding under the TV bench—to come out fighting again or make himself at home; and he seemed to have decided on the latter. His eyes were just as peaceful as they always had been when I had first gotten to know him in the shed, and he strolled around the room before giving us both a long look.

Why are you making such a fuss? he seemed to say. *I'm fine now. No need to worry.*

Ben sniffed the air before padding softly toward George. Turning his body lengthways, Ben started rubbing up against George's legs, back and forth, back and forth. How was George going to react to being touched? I didn't want him to frighten Ben by shooing him away.

George didn't flinch or push Ben away, rub himself to get rid of the feeling of being touched or shout to be left alone, though. He sat completely still until Ben walked away. I wondered if it was a one-off or the start of something new.

I found out for sure the next day after I left George lying on the sofa watching a film with his blue blanket covering him—the blanket that no one else was ever allowed to touch. When I walked back in a few minutes later, I saw Ben stretched out across George, lying on the blanket as though it was a sun lounger on a Spanish beach, while George looked as though it was completely ordinary to be cuddling a cat.

"Ben loves the telly, Mum," he told me.

"Does he?"

"Yeah. He wants to watch *Pokémon*. He wants to see *Peter Pan*. He was in *Peter Pan*."

"Can he fly?"

"Yes. He's good at flying. He's met Tinkerbell and Superman too. He's been on TV lots."

And it was in that moment that I realized Ben wasn't just a cat. He was something far, far more.

Chapter 8

Have you ever met a cat who likes bouncing on trampolines or eating ice cream? Who tires itself out playing hide and seek before getting into bed and lying on its back with its paws in the air? I hadn't until I met Ben, and if someone had told me before that a cat could do all those things, I'd have thought they were a bit touched in the head. But Ben did them. And more.

From that first day when we let him out of the loo and he cuddled up against George, Ben stuck to him like glue. He was more like a dog than a cat: there was nothing cool and collected about him, none of the reserve for which cats are famous. Ben was like a faithful puppy, who followed George from the moment he got up in the morning to the moment he climbed the stairs at night to go to bed. Even then, Ben would follow to watch me tuck George in, and however many times I got up in the night to see to him, he'd be there beside me. When George got up the next morning, he would always find Ben sitting in the same place on the same chair in my bedroom. He would have a good stretch when George came to collect him, before following him into the bathroom when George went to brush his teeth. Then he'd patrol up and down the bed as I got George dressed before meowing for a final cuddle just as George was going out of the door to school.

It was the same every day. Ben seemed to understand how much George needed routine and gave it to him from the moment he arrived. He was a real home cat too, happy in our little house and garden, and once again it was just what George needed. He'd gotten very panicked the first time we'd let Ben out into the garden.

"He might run away, he might run away," he'd chanted as we opened the door.

But Ben had just walked out on to the grass, strolled down to the end and had a look around before running back inside, jumping on to the sofa and curling up for a sleep. He didn't go out again for two days, and when he did it was just for a quick sniff around the garden or into the summer-house, where he would sit for hours. He didn't want to go any farther and most of the time George was the one who ended up persuading him outside for a play by running up to the window and calling him when we were out in the garden.

George's favorite game by now was bouncing on a trampoline I'd bought him after we moved. I really wasn't sure that Ben should join him on it when I first saw them jumping up and down together. Ben's stitches had healed and he was on the mend, but he should still probably have been having a bit more peace and quiet. George could be rough when he played and never stopped when things got out of hand.

"I don't think we can have this," I called as I walked out into the garden. "It can't be very nice for Ben."

George immediately sat down and did not move another muscle. I was beginning to realize that I was going to have to get used to expecting the unexpected now that Ben was around.

"Is you OK, Baboo?" he said in his singsong cat voice. "Is you liking being on the trampoline with me?"

Now George had always worried about Lewis—first about his oxygen tubes, and then as Lewis had gotten older and other kids had laughed at him because he was small, he would cover Lewis's ears so that he didn't hear the jokes. But he'd never actually talked about it or asked how Lewis felt in the way he was doing now with Ben.

"Do you or don't you like bouncing?" he asked him. "Is it making you nervous?"

Ben didn't look as though he wanted to get off the trampoline, but I still wasn't convinced.

"I think it's time for him to get down," I said as George stroked him.

Ben looked at George and then up at me, fixing me with his green eyes. *Leave us alone. Can't you see that we're playing? George and I just want to have fun.*

I wasn't quite sure what to do. I must be going soft if I was listening to a cat. I couldn't let George fling Ben 4 feet in the air, however much they both seemed to enjoy it.

"I don't think he can really like trampolining, and the rubber will get ruined if he puts claw marks in it," I said as I lifted Ben off the trampoline.

"He wouldn't do that."

"I don't think he'd be able to help himself, George."

I put Ben on the ground beside me and he was still for about a second. Then he leaned back into a crouch and jumped back on to the trampoline with a flick of his tail.

You see! Ben seemed to tell me. *I want to play. Don't interrupt us, please. We're having fun!*

I knew when I was beaten. "OK, then, but be gentle."

George started off slowly enough but was soon jumping in the air, with Ben bouncing just as high.

"He's smiling," George shouted as he flew upward and I could see with my own eyes that it was true: as Ben took off into the air, the corners of his mouth were curling up.

Over the next few days, it was the same whatever game George played: nothing worried Ben. After all the hissing and spitting when he was living in the shed, I'd wondered whether he might claw George if things got out of hand. But Ben never reacted to what George did—whether it was grabbing his tail or fiddling with his ears. He just padded calmly around after George, and when George had left for school, Ben would spend the day quietly at home until he heard the sound of the front door, when he ran to meet him.

"Baboo!" George would say as he got down to pet Ben.

The easiness between them was like a gift from some-one up high, because George's relaxed behavior with Ben was a huge contrast to how things were at school. By the time Ben arrived they'd gotten so bad that George was at risk of being excluded, and as I was called in again and again I was worried sick. I knew Miss Proctor was doing all she could, and George had also started working with a teaching assistant called Ms. Bahsin, who he had responded to well. Together with Miss Proctor, she had tried every trick up her sleeve to get George to learn. After realizing how much he liked shiny things, if he worked well Ms. Bahsin started rewarding him with little gifts like a ball covered in silver glitter; to encourage him and build his confidence, Ms. Bahsin and Miss Proctor made him charts covered in stickers; and to help him mix with other children, they gave him special play special sessions in the soft play area with just a couple of kids. Even so, George's behavior at school had gotten worse.

"I've got ADHD," George would say again and again after picking up on conversations around him and if I asked him to look at a book with me, he'd tell me he couldn't because he didn't know how to read and write like other children.

You see, George knew he was different because of how people reacted to him and the worst place for that was the playground. It wasn't so much the children but the mums, who would gasp as he shouted swear words he'd learned or pushed into people as he ran out of the playground, and George couldn't help but know he was being talked about. I knew there were two Georges: the one who wanted to make other children from the special needs unit happy by pushing them so fast around the playground in their wheelchairs that they screamed with laughter, and the other who ran wild as anger exploded out of him—which was the George most people saw.

"He's out of control, that kid," I'd hear mothers mutter as I walked past and they gave me icy looks.

"If he goes near my Casey I'm going to the teachers."

"Have you heard his language?"

The playground felt like a war zone in which I had to do battle, day in and day out, and even though I tried to ignore the whispers, there's only so thick-skinned you can be, isn't there? Each day I'd walk in with a grin fixed on my face and say a cheery "hello" to anyone who looked my way, but even the two mums who could see things weren't right with George and were prepared to chat with me stopped after he had a fight with one of their little boys. I must have gotten distracted for a few seconds as we walked into school, because I looked up to see George pinning the boy to the ground.

"George, no!" I cried as I pulled him off, unable to understand where his rage had suddenly sprung from.

The boy's mum was rigid with anger as she looked at me, and we were soon both called in to see a teacher.

"George is a bully," the mum kept saying. "I've heard all the stories and look what he's done now! '

All I could do was apologize again and again, but the mum wouldn't listen. From that day on, she never spoke a word to me again.

"I don't understand," I told the teacher later. "I thought George and that boy got on OK."

"They do sometimes," she said. "But most of the children are wary of him. They keep their distance."

How can words like that not break your heart? Eventually we got to the bottom of the problem and found out that the little boy George had fought with had been taking his Pokémon cards. It didn't make what George had done right, but at least there was a reason why he'd done what he'd done. No one wanted to hear it, though: George was trouble, and the parents kept themselves and their kids away from us. We started using a separate entrance to get in and out of school because it was felt it would be better for George—and everyone else.

So that was why Ben arrived at just the right time to give George what he needed most when he needed it most: acceptance. Ben liked George for who he was and I'd never known how much he needed that until he started to blossom before my eyes—just as I'd never known how deep my longing was to see him happy. It was like an ache that had settled so deeply into my bones over the years that I'd gotten used to it. When I started to hear George's laughter with Ben, the pain finally started to ease.

Ben was a colorful character with as many likes and dislikes as any person. When it came to food, he loved chicken, ham, toast with butter, salmon and mash, hot dogs and a lick of George's ice cream. He hated tinned food almost as much as he disliked the noise of a Hoover, which made him run as if a pack of wild dogs were chasing him. What he loved most of all, though, apart from people, was warmth—a patch of sunlight in the summerhouse, the top of a radiator or a pile of clothes just out of the tumble drier would do. He even started getting into my bed. Although we'd tried putting Ben in his own basket on the landing outside our bedrooms when he'd first arrived, he wasn't having any of it. Ben had a will like iron and when it came to meowing outside a closed door he would carry on for hours, starting off with a soft whine and getting louder and louder until he sounded like a screaming baby. George had wanted Ben in bed with him, of course, but he woke him up too much, so I was the one who'd given in. Soon Ben had his own pillow on the empty side of my bed and would lie on it beside me, only getting up when I did. Most mornings I would wake up to find Ben stretched out on his back with his legs in the air and when I moved, he would open his eyes and look at me.

This is the life, isn't it, Ju? All lovely and cozy. What a good sleep I've had!

The worst thing in the world for Ben was to sleep alone because it wasn't warm. As I got to know him, I couldn't understand how he'd lived outside for so long. He hated the cold so much that he refused to go out in the rain and we had to walk him into the garden with an umbrella. Maybe he'd been the Queen of Sheba or something in a former life because Ben loved to be adored. If he was sitting on the sofa and George dared stop stroking him, Ben would cry for more until his belly was rubbed again and he'd lie back contentedly as he watched TV. He always enjoyed TV, but whenever Katie Price appeared on the television his eyes became even more glued and he'd sit completely still as he watched her. Ben was fast becoming the most spoiled cat in London with a taste for glam celebrities.

There were two sides to Ben and the one I saw most was the wise old man with the peaceful eyes. After George had gone off to school, Ben would climb into my arms for a cuddle and gaze calmly at me until I finally got up to do some jobs around the house and he'd settle down for a sleep. Soon enough, though, he'd come to find me again, because there was only so long that Ben could go without a bit of love and if he felt he'd been ignored for too long, he'd make sure someone soon took notice of him. If I was out in the garden, he'd sit himself down in the middle of the bed I was digging and fix me with a look; when I tried to look something up on the computer, Ben would lie on the keyboard; if I laid the table for a meal, he would jump up on to it.

It's been a whole hour since you stroked me! This isn't good enough. I want a cuddle.

It wasn't just George and I who had to adore Ben. If anyone came to visit, he wanted to be the center of attention. If Boy arrived with my nephews and nieces—Harry, William, Chloe and Frank—Ben would clamber up a tree on the drive to watch them arrive. After giving us just long enough to say hello, he'd start running around to make sure we stopped and took notice of him. When Mum came over and we sat out on the patio, Ben would roll around on the floor until she tickled him or sit with his head held high as we chatted to make sure we knew he was part of the conversation. As we talked, he would move his head from side to side to look at whoever was speaking; I really wouldn't have been all that surprised if he'd cleared his throat one day and said a few words himself.

Although Ben was small, he was able to command a room's attention, and although our friends and family all liked cats, even the strangers who didn't so much had to give in to him. When a social worker came to see me about George, Ben climbed on to her lap and sat slap bang in the middle of her paperwork. The woman went a bit stiff as he looked at her, but Ben meowed to let her know that she had no choice but to stroke him. He also came out whenever I was talking to someone on the drive and would wind around our legs until he was noticed. He soon became a favorite with all the pensioners who lived in the bungalows nearby. He'd sit on the drive when the sun was shining, waiting for them to walk past to the post office or to do a bit of shopping. "Hello, Ben," they'd coo as he ran up to them and pushed against their legs with pleasure as they bent stiffly down to him.

But as much as Ben loved people, he had eyes only for George when he was around. It was as though no one else existed and the wise old grandpa I knew who crept softly about most of the day was transformed into an energetic little boy who whizzed around from the moment George arrived home. Even though the vet had told me he thought Ben was about six years old, which is almost middle aged for a cat, he could still be like a kitten when he wanted to be. His favorite game was hide and seek. If he and George had been sitting down too long, Ben would suddenly jump up before running off to give the signal that he wanted to be chased.

"I'm coming," George would shout as he raced upstairs after Ben, who could usually be found hiding under a bed or wardrobe.

The moment he was spotted, Ben would bomb off to hide again and the game would start all over. He and George spent hours playing it together.

Their other favorite was a toy wand with a cuddly mouse attached to it on a rubber string. Each evening, about an hour before George's bedtime, Ben would look at him.

Come on, George. I'm bored. Let's play. Why don't you show me the mouse?

So George would get up, pick up the wand and Ben

would stare at it, still as a statue, until George flicked it for the first time. Then Ben would go mad, jumping and scurrying around as the mouse went flying, diving and rolling to get it while George laughed his head off. George played with Ben so easily and freely that he didn't even mind when he made a mess of things. If George played with another child and they knocked over one of his plastic figures of knights and pirates, he would lift the whole board above his head, drop it and walk away without a backward glance. But that never happened with Ben—instead if Ben got in the way he'd laugh.

"You want to win, don't you, Baboo?" he'd cry before putting the figures back in line.

It did not take the two of them long to discover their other favorite game, the sandpit. I walked out into the garden one day to find George sitting in it, building a castle. When he'd finished, he sat back on his heels and waited as Ben slowly uncurled himself, got to his feet and walked without a care in the world before lying down on top of the castle. George started laughing as the sand crumbled beneath Ben.

"Baboo!" George said in cat talk. "What is you doing?"

The game went on and on and George couldn't get enough of it, but no matter how many times he wanted to repeat a game, Ben would play. He never refused to move or got bored, and woe betide anyone, or anything, that tried to get in the way of their fun—like an earwig George spotted in the sandpit one day.

"Baboo!" he cried, running into the living room and picking up Ben.

George took him out into the garden and pointed at the

earwig scurrying around in the sand.

"Get it!" he cried.

As George stared, Ben fixed the earwig in his sights and started jabbing at it with his paw as he chased it, leaping about after the tiny bug as he tried to catch it.

"Go on, Ben," George cried. "You can get it."

Ben darted around, eyes locked on the intruder. But it was so quick that every time he smashed his paw down, the earwig reappeared and made another run for it. George and I started howling with laughter as we watched Ben dance around, jumping up and down, backward and forward, until his paw smashed into the sand for a final time. He'd got it! Ben scooped up the earwig in his paw and popped it into his mouth.

Delicious!

"You is so good," George said with a smile.

I couldn't help but wonder where the cat had been all my life. It had only been a few weeks but already our life had changed in so many ways. Ben was opening a door inside George and as we walked through it together, we were discovering a new world.

"There's a bird in the house," George yelled as I got out of the car.

My heart sank. I knew what this meant. In less than a month, I'd learned that Ben liked to give presents—dead or alive. Ever since he'd arrived, I'd regularly found mice that had been skewered by his sharp claws and left on our living-room floor as a gift. One day he'd even brought home a frog, after finding it in the small pond in our garden. All the goldfish had been taken by herons, so we didn't think there was much left in the water. But Ben had managed to find the one thing that had survived the massacre, and I'd got the fright of my life as I got up to turn off the television one night and a frog jumped across the room. Ben had flung himself on the floor, ready to pounce, as I screamed blue murder and George jumped on to the sofa. In the end I'd phoned Nob, who came over and caught the frog because I was too petrified to do it. Ben had looked at me in disgust as the frog was taken back out into the garden.

Why don't you like my present, Julia? That frog was hard to catch and now you've gone and let it go again.

George was just as squeamish as me and what scared us both the most was when Ben brought home mice that were still alive but petrified. If George and I saw one in the house, we'd get on to the sofa to get our feet up off the floor and call Nob again. He'd even had to come out at midnight once because I knew I'd never sleep knowing that a mouse was loose in the house. Nob had trapped it in a jar and taken it out into the garden while George and I waited.

"All done," he said as he came back into the house. "Can I go back to bed, please?"

But now as I stood on the drive with George, I knew that Nob wouldn't be able to help us, because he was at work. There was just me, George and my neighbor, Wendy, who had been looking after George while I nipped out to get a pint of milk. I'd gotten to know her well because she lived a few doors down with her husband, Keith, and daughters, Nicky and Kayleigh. At first, I'd doubted I'd find another friend like Michelle when I moved because although we'd kept in touch, our lives were both busy and we didn't see as much of each other anymore. But when I started chatting with Wendy, I knew I'd met another of those rare people who took George in their stride.

"Kayleigh's hyper," George would tell her as we talked on the doorstep. "Keith hasn't got no hair."

"That's right, George," Wendy would reply without batting an eyelid.

Over time we'd become such good friends that George even let Wendy come into the house to keep an eye on him if I had to go out for a short while. I still couldn't leave him with her for long, though, and had had to come home from the hospital after a minor operation, although the doctor had wanted me to stay in overnight. If I was gone too long George would start to worry and he would get anxious that his routines weren't going right. The fact that he'd let Wendy come into the house, though, was a step forward in itself.

I stared at Wendy, wondering what I was going to do about the storm that had erupted in the house while I was out.

"It's a baby magpie," she told me and I knew I had to save the poor thing from Ben's claws.

As I started walking toward the front door, George ran after me.

"Baboo is going crazy," he shrieked. "The bird's got away from him, but he's going to get out his wings and take it prisoner. Ben can fly like a plane. He was a jet pilot once."

George was using cat talk like this more and more now. In his cartoon voice, he had started telling me about all the imaginary adventures Ben went on. I loved hearing about them because George had never been able to talk to me like this. Ben was helping him to say things he never had before and I knew that George was also using cat talk to tell me things he'd learned. I'd never known if he'd taken in what I and other people had tried to teach him over the years—from historical facts to lessons about right and wrong—but now George showed me that he had. He'd also picked up all sorts of other bits of throwaway information as well.

"Ben's been on a Slim Shake diet three times a day but he's cheating because I see him eat all the Twix," George would say and I knew he'd noticed that I'd been trying to cut down on what I ate for years.

"You need to go to Weight Watchers," he'd tell Ben as he picked off the bits of leaves and grass that collected on the soft white fur on Ben's stomach, and it made me giggle to hear him mention what he'd heard Mum and me chatting about.

However many times I told him, though, that Ben's low-slung stomach was the result of being neutered years before, George was convinced he had a weight problem. Ben had a tummy so big it picked up bits of dirt and George had to brush it. Ben loved it when George groomed him, because keeping clean was very important to him. He could spend hours letting George brush him, and when there wasn't someone around to pamper him, Ben would devote almost a whole morning to licking his ears. His paws were his prize possession, though. The back ones looked as if he was wearing white socks that stretched up to his knee, the front two had just a slip of white on them like baby booties, and Ben always made sure they were clean. But when he followed George upstairs to keep watch on him as he had a bath, Ben would get teased.

"Is your teeth yellow?" George would say excitedly as

Ben lay in the sink, which was his favorite spot from which to watch bathtime. "Do you clean your teeth? Have you washed behind your ears and under your arms?"

The only thing that tempted Ben out of the sink was George blowing bubbles on to the floor, because he loved to chase them.

"I ain't got yellow teeth!" George would say for Ben. "I'm a very clean cat. It's you who's the smelly one, George."

"I'm not smelly!" George would cry. "I wash with the soap and I'm clean as a whistle."

It made me laugh so much to hear the kinds of phrases that George had picked up. In his conversations with Ben he could thread all he had heard into his rich imagination.

"Go outside!" George would tell me excitedly. "Baboo's on the roof. He's going to do a parachute jump. He's been mending all the roofs. Putting on new ones with his hammer."

As George spoke, I would see the pictures of Ben in my head that he had painted for me with his words and start giggling as I imagined Ben dressed as a lumberjack with a hammer and tools or wearing a pilot's uniform. Sometimes we could lose ourselves for hours imagining Ben's adventures, and I could hardly remember how silent the house had been before he arrived. Our days were full of talk and laughter now, and George's happiness was beginning to stretch from day to day, week to week, as he used Ben to tell me the things he couldn't bring himself to say directly—the thoughts he had, the feelings, the stories that constantly filled his imagination.

Ben was such a constant presence for us both that he

was with us even when he wasn't, because we talked about him all the time when we were out.

"Ben tried out these safety straps," George told me as we got on a ride at an amusement park during one of the trips that I still took him on, just as I had done since he was young. "And when the ride starts, he'll come out and slap the kids on the head."

We started giggling as the roller coaster moved slowly to a start.

"I can't believe he's got a day job!" I exclaimed.

"Yes, he has. He works on security. He made this ride for me, he did. It's his favorite."

Ben could be anything George wanted him to be and I loved hearing about what he imagined for him. But it wasn't all make-believe: sometimes George used cat talk to tell me things that he wanted to say to me—from something that had made him smile to an incredible fact he'd heard on the television.

Cat talk wasn't going to help us now, though, as I stood on the drive with George and Wendy; the magpie inside the house was all too real. Ben was chasing the bird even as we wondered what to do, and I had to rescue it. Taking a deep breath, I walked into the house and opened the living-room door.

The magpie was flapping wildly about, with Ben prancing about underneath.

What a beautiful present I've brought you. Look at the bird! It's great, isn't it?

All I could think of as Ben stared at the magpie with pride was that old Hitchcock film *The Birds*. I slammed the door shut and walked outside.

"Are you scared?" Wendy asked when she saw my face, the color of chalk.

I didn't say a word.

"I'll sort it out for you," Wendy told me bravely. "I just need a pair of gloves. No need to panic."

I ran into the kitchen to get her some rubber gloves and Wendy pulled them on to her hands with a face like a surgeon getting ready to go into the operating theater.

"You two wait here," she said, and disappeared inside.

Five seconds later, Wendy ran out of the front door. "I don't think I can do it," she said. "I'll go and get Keith."

I wasn't sure the poor bird could take much more of this. There was blood on the front door where it must have flown into it in panic, and I hated thinking of Ben torturing the poor thing. For a loving cat, he certainly had a nasty streak. But Keith saved the day: he came over, caught the magpie and took it out into the back garden, where it flew away.

"You are so naughty, Ben," I cried after we'd gone back into the house and George had picked him up.

But as I leaned toward Ben to give him a stern look, he nipped me with his teeth.

Don't tell me off, Julia! I was only bringing you a present. Why are you angry? I was just trying to be nice!

As I looked at Ben sitting in George's arms, I knew that I wasn't going to change him. I was just going to have to accept that Ben had his quirks—as everyone does. He was so much more than his little misdemeanors. Look at George and me: we were talking to each other in a way we never had before, and it was all because of Ben. He had given us voices and even if they were high, cartoon and just a little bit crazy, I did not mind. Now I could return the favor. If Ben loved rodents and birds a bit too much, or didn't like it when I told him off, I would just have to let him be.

Chapter 9

George had made another friend as well as Ben: a little boy called Arthur, who lived next door with his mum and was one of those kids who thought everything over before he did it, a 10-year-old going on 55. Arthur was patient and kind, and he didn't pay too much attention when George shouted that he'd had enough if Arthur didn't do what he wanted as they played. He just went home without a backward glance and came back cheerful as ever the next day.

I was sure that the playful side Ben had brought out so much in George was what helped him become such good friends with Arthur. The seeds for it had been sown even before Ben arrived when Howard bought George a computer after we moved. He loved all the games so much he even started playing them over the Internet with people from other countries. I didn't know what to make of it when George told me he was one of the best in the world at one particular game because I couldn't even work the TV control properly. Then Howard told me George wasn't too far off the mark and I realized I shouldn't have been surprised, because it was a world in which George didn't have to interact with people face to face. Even so, as I listened to George talk over the Internet—because you can never be too careful—I noticed that he was laughing and joking with people more and more.

"How old are you?" I'd hear a voice from America or Australia ask George.

"Ten," he'd reply.

"Ten? Really, man? You're only ten?"

George would giggle as he listened and every now and again he'd tell whoever he was talking to that he was 33, just to make himself laugh a bit more. He was a great mimic and could do all the accents as he repeated what he'd heard.

Ben brought out that playfulness even more and when George finally showed it to Arthur, it felt as though he'd won a marathon after all those years of trying to get over the starting line with other kids.

For the first few months they were friends, Arthur and George played computer games and watched TV, or spent hours in the garden on the trampoline together, bouncing so high that once Arthur ended up getting stuck in a rose that climbed up the fence. He had thorn scratches all over his head by the time I untangled him.

George came to have a look. "Would you like some sweets?" he asked Arthur. "They'll make you feel better."

Arthur didn't say anything as I steadied him on his feet. He just rubbed his head and looked at the rose.

"Shall I make you laugh?" George asked him. "Shall I jump in the rose too?"

With that, Arthur started giggling. "Don't do that, George," he told him. "Why don't we just have some lemonade or something?"

Ben wasn't quite sure what to make of Arthur at first, and when Arthur came over to play, he'd often sit inside and just watch the boys together. But every now and again he would join them on the trampoline; and Ben certainly wasn't going to let George out of his sight when he started exploring with Arthur. I suppose I should have known that George would want to go farther than our garden one day. But I still felt nervous when he asked if he and Arthur could go on to the recreation field opposite our house. A lot of kids went there to play football or climb trees, but I'd never let George leave the house without me before. Although I knew I had to let George have a little bit of independence, it's hard to give it to a child who you just want to stick to you like glue. He knew, though, that other children his age went out to play without their parents, just as I knew that I couldn't keep him locked in the little world we had with Ben—just the three of us—forever.

Two things finally convinced me to let George go out. One was Arthur. Just as some adults never grow up, there are children like Arthur who are old before their years and his middle name should have been "sensible." I'd never had to sit Arthur down and explain George's autism to him; he just understood that he had to look out for George. The second was that the recreation field was directly opposite my kitchen window, so I'd know if George wandered off from Arthur; I told George this, and that I would stop him going out again if he did. Whenever they went on to the field, I would conveniently do the washing up so that I could watch George like an undercover James Bond spy to make sure he was OK. I had an extra pair of eyes too, because Ben always followed and if George went out to play or took his remote-controlled car on to the field, Ben would lie on the pavement keeping watch on him.

As Arthur and George ventured out together, I saw for myself that George was having fun as he kicked the football or climbed trees, with Ben following not far behind most of the time. One day when they went out to play with Arthur's cousin Charlie I even packed up a lunch for them, and they had a great time—until disaster struck when George decided to jump out of a tree. My heart was in my mouth when Arthur and Charlie came running to tell me that George was stuck on a fence. I ran to the field to find him hanging off the fence by his collar. As I lifted him off, I wondered if I'd ever be able to let him out again.

"The children in the park said, 'I dare you to jump,'" George told me when we got him home. "So I thought I'd see if I could. I tried to jump toward the green grass."

Arthur looked sternly at George as he spoke. "You can't jump out of trees, George," he said. "Because you might hurt your legs and then how would you play football? Why would you want to do that—whatever anyone says?"

George bent down to Ben, who was sitting beside him on the sofa. "Hear that?" he said. "You mustn't jump out of trees, Ben. It's naughty."

I couldn't help but think back to the day so long ago when Michelle and I had used the eggs to try to teach George how fragile he was. Now finally he seemed to understand—even though it had taken jumping out of a tree to teach him—and I was so relieved as George spoke to Ben, who meowed as he talked.

"Don't laugh," George said, using the same kind of serious voice with Ben that Arthur had just used with him. "It's not funny."

I got the feeling that George wouldn't be jumping out of anymore trees soon.

That day cemented the boys' friendship. George was soon as protective of Arthur as he was of Lewis, and if someone dared say a word against Arthur he would tell them off.

"He is the best footballer," he'd say if a child made a joke about Arthur. "He's fantastic. He's really good at goals."

George hero-worshipped his friend and would have given him the clothes off his back if Arthur had asked for them. But Arthur never took advantage of George's trust in him.

"Would you like the chocolates Nan gave me for my birthday?" George would ask. "Do you want my Pokémon cards?"

"All those things cost a lot of money," Arthur would tell George as they played on the computer. "So why not just give me one chocolate instead of the whole box?"

George would hand it over and look the other way as Arthur took it.

"You're my best friend," George would tell him as he stared into the distance, and then they'd go back to their game without another word.

My heart would swell every time I heard George say that. I know most mums take things like that for granted by the time their child is 10. But I'd never had those kinds of milestones with George before—his first real friend and the forming of a bond between them—and I felt so excited that he was finally showing who he really was, revealing the loving and kind little boy inside him.

There were fallings out, of course. George still found it hard to let people do their own thing and would shout at Arthur sometimes when their game didn't go as he wanted it to. But the only time Arthur really got angry was when George told him off for dropping litter.

"Don't you care about the world?" George exclaimed when Arthur threw a disposable cup on the floor. "Do you know that the earth is being filled up with plastic?"

That caused a bit of upset, because Arthur didn't like George telling him what was what, but they made up in the end. Tellings off like that were George's new thing now. After all the years of my drumming manners into him, he'd learned how important they were and would tell a child when they did something he thought was rude—however many times I told him that people didn't always like being told what to do.

"Someone needs to tell them, Mum," George would say. "They need to learn. They're out of control, they are."

I couldn't help but smile when he told me that. George had always been convinced that it was the world around him that was topsy-turvy, not him. He had a point, though, because some of the kids on our estate ran a bit wild. But I stopped myself from giggling too much as I told George that the other kids might not like it when he told them off. That was life with George: like being on a pinball machine, because as soon as you hit one target you were pinged on to the next.

Most kids couldn't understand it when George told them what was what or said their mum's teeth stuck out. But Arthur liked George for who he was and I was happy that George liked Arthur just as much back. Life is all about the small steps forward which together help you walk the distance, and George's friendship with Arthur felt like a leap forward that Ben had helped him make.

Ben was getting more and more territorial. It had taken a while for him to work out how far his kingdom stretched, but when he did, he wouldn't stand for anyone trying to invade it.

He'd always known that Fluffy the rabbit was part of the household and even though I was a bit worried he might try to nip her, Ben never took any notice of her. "She's Ben's pet," George would tell me. "Fluffy is his. He don't like cats because he's got allergies. But he likes Fluffy." In the end, I'd sit Fluffy in the garden for a bit of a sunbathe sometimes and Ben would just stretch out beside her. He seemed to think, just as George did, that he wasn't a cat at all, so why on earth would a rabbit interest him?

But it wasn't as simple with other animals, and the gentle nature Ben showed Fluffy disappeared when it came to dogs or other cats. They were the two things guaranteed to bring out Ben's fighting spirit and the loving, gentle cat we knew was transformed into a ninja warrior.

After rescuing Ben, I'd taken pity on a few more stray cats and fed them. Most disappeared almost as quickly as they arrived, but a couple had become regular visitors and I gave them a meal almost every day. One was a tabby boy who I left out a bowl for in the back garden, just as I had once done for Ben; another was a beautiful fluffy girl, who was the Oliver Twist of my foster pets because she was always peering through the kitchen window and asking for more food. But although Ben just about tolerated both our visitors as long as they stayed outside the house, it was another matter if they tried putting a paw through his front door.

"You need to be kind to them," George would tell him as Ben hissed if one of the strays tried to come over the threshold. "You lived on the streets and you was as hungry as them once, weren't you?"

But Ben would just shoot him an angry glare and run off to take refuge on the sofa.

This is my house, George. Mine. And I don't want anyone else in it. Don't you understand? I don't like other cats.

Most of the time, we managed to avoid trouble, but then came the day when the tabby, who we'd nicknamed Buster, decided to explore a bit more. By now, Ben had made the summerhouse his very own and where once I'd sat gazing out at my garden, Ben had now taken up residency. If he wasn't in the living room or on a bed, he could always be found sitting in the summerhouse. From there he could keep a close eye on everything that was going on.

George and I were picking tomatoes on the day that Buster crept down the garden toward the door into the living room. Ben was asleep. At least he seemed to be, until his eyes snapped open the moment the tabby went past the summerhouse and narrowed as Buster took another few steps toward the house. Quick as a flash, Ben jumped off his chair and ran out on to the lawn with his hair on end and growling like a lion.

Get out of here! Get away! Don't you dare go into my house!

Ben ran full tilt at Buster, who turned around to see his enemy steaming down the garden like a freight train. Buster took one look, pushed back his ears and ran for cover as Ben hissed and spat. After taking a flying leap up the fence, Buster was gone. George and I stood open mouthed, our hands full of tomatoes. George laughed as Ben scampered proudly back up the garden with his head held high and his tail swishing behind him. Ben looked pleased as punch with himself as he settled down on the edge of the patio to make sure Buster didn't try another raid.

Ben's victory that day soon made him so confident that he wanted to extend the boundaries of his kingdom, and one very odd addition to it was my car. Whenever I cleaned it, Ben would come out, climb inside, hop on to the dashboard and stare out the windscreen at passersby. As music played from the car stereo and George and I covered everything in suds, Ben would watch us.

Good job. Keep going. I think you've missed a bit just over there, haven't you?

Even when he was inside, Ben was determined to keep an eye on his territory, which caused all sorts of problems. I got through two bedroom blinds because he broke the slats by pushing his head through them one too many times. A pair of curtains didn't do much better when Ben ripped them with his claws as he ran up them; it was just the same with the kitchen blind. Ben was like a watchman on permanent guard, and even when he gave himself a bit of time off, he caused another kind of havoc by digging his claws into anything from the sofa to the carpet to the chair legs. I regularly walked into the living room to find him flexing his long claws, his fur fluffed up and his eyes so dazed with pleasure that he looked drunk as a skunk as he dug into the fabric with a look of ecstasy. To Ben, ripping up my soft furnishings was like reaching nirvana. Buying him a scratching pole didn't do any good because it wasn't nearly as much fun.

"Will you stop it!" I'd cry when I came into the lounge to find Ben plunging his claws into the rug again or teasing another run of fabric pulls into the edge of the sofa.

But George would always defend his friend. "Those scratching poles are for cats, so they're not for Ben," he'd tell me. "He likes the rug, so why can't we just buy a new one when it's too old?"

"Because money doesn't grow on trees," I'd exclaim. "I can't go buying new sofas and carpets and curtains and blinds just because Ben wants to claw them."

"Oh, Mum," George would tell me. "Ben loves doing it and you only live once, don't you?"

I knew that George would never see my point and I swear that whenever we talked about this tricky subject, Ben would sit down beside him and look at me with a satisfied smile.

You can't tell me off, you know. I'm George's cat and he's so nice he'll let me do just what I want. Give up, Julia. I like the sofa far too much to leave it alone.

But although Ben's naughtiness caused problems, I could not help but laugh most of the time, because he was so fearless about it all. While the cats he chased off were about his size and weight, Ben didn't seem to even consider that the dogs he teased were twice the size of him. After cats, they were his next best enemy. While he had tolerated Mum's dogs, Oli and Sally, when he first arrived by just ignoring them, Ben slowly showed his true fighting colors. Sitting on the window ledge outside the living room, he would stare in at Sally and Oli when they visited with a look of such concentration that we'd laugh: it was as if he was trying to hypnotize them.

But Ben's patience finally snapped when I had a dog to stay and he decided enough was enough as far as canine intruders were concerned.

When Arthur and his mum went on holiday, I agreed to look after their British bulldog called Jedi. I'd always liked him: Jedi was so sweet natured that he let himself be wrapped in blankets like a baby when he got cold and he liked nothing more than getting into the passenger seat of the car beside me when I went out shopping. But all Ben wanted to do was intimidate our house guest. Jedi could not even wee in peace because Ben would follow him outside and stare so hard that poor Jedi couldn't perform. All I could do to help was follow them into the garden every time Jedi wanted to do the necessary, but all hell broke loose one afternoon when Jedi slipped out unseen.

"Ben's going riding," I heard George shout and I ran into the living room to see Jedi running in.

He was twisting and flipping around as he tried to get something off his back—a long black shadow, a streak of white fur: a cat. Ben was clinging on to Jedi's back as though he was riding a bucking bronco.

"Let go," I screamed. "Get off the poor dog."

But Ben wasn't in any mood to let go. He dug his claws in even further as Jedi gave a yelp and ran out into the garden, where he carried on desperately trying to shake off his attacker. As Ben clung on for dear life, Jedi did a final huge shake and managed to dislodge him. Ben flew into the air and the moment he landed on his feet assumed the attack position. Jedi, realizing he was free at last, lay on the ground and gave me a bewildered look from between his paws as Ben started scampering around. He might have been shaken off by Jedi but he'd still managed to frighten him out of his wits. That was a victory for Ben and it only gave him a taste for more.

When Jedi went home at the end of the week, Ben would sit in a tree on our drive, waiting for him to leave the house for a walk. Most of the time he just stared menacingly, but once he took a flying leap at Jedi from the branches; and when a Staffordshire bull terrier made the mistake of stepping on to our drive, Ben reared up on his hind legs and started slapping the dog's face with his paws.

The defense of his realm was not only practical, though: it was pleasurable. When Ben realized just how much fun it was to tease dogs he soon found the perfect victim: Wendy's Yorkshire terrier, Scruffy. During the summer, Wendy often put a baby gate across her lounge door to keep him safe inside while she opened the front door to let air through the house. When Ben realized that Scruffy was behind bars, he'd walk up the drive whenever he saw Wendy's door open, sit down on the step and stare into the house. Every time a coconut, Scruffy would go wild and jump up and down as he tried to get over the baby gate to reach Ben. Scruffy was so small, of course, that he was never going to manage it, but Ben relished every moment of tormenting him. He never stepped foot in Wendy's house or got too near poor Scruffy. Instead he sat just out of reach, staring in and driving Scruffy wild.

But as much as Ben had a blind spot when it came to other cats and dogs, I slowly learned that he was far more objective about people. At first I'd thought that he was a really friendly cat, because Ben loved all the people George and I liked best in the world: when Mum came over, he'd run to her for a pickup; when Nob, Tor or Boy arrived, he'd roll over to have his tummy scratched; and if Wendy knocked on the door, he'd run to it so fast that I thought he might smash his way through to the other side.

But as the months went on, I began to realize that he was far more selective than that. You know those people who always seem to have a problem and need endless cups of tea while they talk it over? I'd met such a woman—we'll call her Sue—who always seemed to be in trouble and I was usually the person she wanted to talk to about it all. Sue would turn up day or night, quite often a bit worse for wear, and I'd sit on the sofa listening while George paced around. He didn't often take against people, but he really didn't like Sue because her fake tan and tattooed eyebrows made her look like a clown to him and he didn't like that at all.

Ben never went near Sue either, and I wondered if I'd ever have the courage to tell her that her visits weren't always welcome. As it happened I didn't get the chance, because one night when Sue turned up and lurched toward George, Ben dug his claws into her, defending his friend, and we never saw Sue again after that night. Maybe it was just a coincidence, but I've always wondered if it was because she realized that her number was up. I'd always been too soft to turn Sue away, but Ben had told her how we all felt in no uncertain terms. As much as I knew he shouldn't go around attacking people, I was just a tiny bit grateful that he'd stood up to Sue on behalf of us all. If only he'd have been a bit nicer to cats and dogs life would have been perfect.

Lots of people have a special voice for their pet. Sometimes it's high and squeaky, sometimes low and gruff. Whether it's dog talk, hamster talk or whatever-pet-it-is-that-they're-chatting-to talk, most use it only when they're alone with the animal, for fear that other people will laugh at them. But I didn't worry about that; George and I used our cat voices to talk about anything and everything under the sun. Cat talk was giving us a happy life, a fun one, and drawing us closer together all the time, so that's why people like Mum, Boy, Nob and Tor heard us cat talking when they came to visit. Instead of wondering if I'd finally lost my marbles, they started using it too when they saw the good it was doing George. Imagine Nob and Boy doing it; one's a cab driver, the other one's a drainage technician for the local council, yet they both spoke in high-pitched voices because they wanted to do anything that would bring George out of himself. None of us understood why cat talk worked, but we could hear for ourselves that it was helping George say things he'd never said before.

"My nan's a pensioner," he'd say in cat talk to Ben when Mum was visiting.

"Yes, I am," she'd reply in her special voice.

"She's old," George would say. "Anything that happens my mum rings her mum because she's a pensioner and knows everything."

Cat talk gave us all a window on to George's world, as he started asking questions—and listening to answers—in a way he'd never done before. Previously when Mum had tried telling him the odd thing about me as a child, George had never responded. Now he laughed when she told him what I'd got up to. He loved hearing how Granddad had once had to bash me on the back when I swallowed a balloon by accident or how I'd tied one of the cups from my plastic tea set to a helium balloon and cried for days when it floated off into the wide blue yonder.

"You should have seen her face," Mum would cry with laughter as George giggled.

Cat talk allowed George to speak about and through Ben, which was easier for him than talking about or as himself. And as we got to the end of our first year with Ben, I began to wonder if I could use it to speak to George about other things as well. Discipline was one thing I decided to see if cat talk could help with. Telling George off had never got either of us anywhere, because many rules just did not make sense to him and over the years I had begun to understand why.

Some rules are clear cut, aren't they? For instance, George had to understand that he could not hurt someone, so when he was little I'd bitten him when he did it to other kids, trodden on his foot when he'd gone through his stamping phase and pulled his hair when he kept tugging on ponytails in the playground. Usually it had taken a couple of years to get George to learn what I was trying to teach him, and I lost count of the times when I'd tried to show him that something hurt—not too much, of course, but just a bit—and he'd lain on the floor telling me to call an ambulance because I'd broken his arm or sprained his foot. But while he learned such rules eventually, with other rules it was harder to teach him, because a lot of them are more about feelings and niceties than black and white facts, so they didn't seem logical to George; explaining those kinds of rules made about as much sense to him as saying that the sky was pink with green spots. Now, though, I had Ben to try to teach George.

I started with burping. George had a terrible habit of doing it really loudly, which had always bothered me because I wanted him to understand manners as much as possible. Whatever I'd said about burping, though—and I'd said a lot over the years—George wouldn't stop doing it, so I decided to try a different approach.

"Ben don't like that," I said one day after George had burped as we sat at the table.

His face didn't flicker as I spoke and he was silent for a minute as he thought.

"Don't he?" George asked eventually.

"No."

"Why?"

"Because he thinks it's rude and Ben don't like being rude."

"Really?"

"Yes. Ben is a very polite cat. He don't agree with burping."

George did not say anything else but soon after that conversation, he started running out of the room to get some toilet paper whenever he wanted to burp. Putting the paper in front of his mouth, he'd still let out a noisy one but it was a start at least. I had to laugh, though, when he began to go that extra George mile with the new thing he'd learned. After realizing that Ben was a very polite cat, he started letting anyone who accidentally burped in front of him know that it wasn't on.

"Ben don't like that," he'd say seriously. "He thinks it's very rude."

Cat talk wasn't just about me communicating better with George: it was about him communicating better with me too. Although he had never been interested in books, George was showing me more and more that he had stories inside him—they just had to be told in a way that didn't use paper and words.

"Do you do or do you don't like sand castles?" George asked Ben as they sat in the sand pit together, Ben looking up at him.

"I do but I love Windsor Castle the most and that don't have any sand," George said as he pretended to be Ben.

"Well, I'm going to build you a castle," George said back to him. "And you must stand on the bucket because if I open the gates then the water will come rushing round the castle and you might get wet feet. OK, mister?"

Once again he replied as Ben. "Well, I do and I don't like getting wet, so don't get me wet, please, George. I only get wet when I wear my diving suit and it's packed for my holiday."

"But don't you like swimming with the fishes under the sea?" George asked him. "I've been and seen them. All the fishes swimming in the blue, blue sea."

Lewis was with us that day and had dressed up in a pirate suit before climbing up on to the trampoline.

George looked solemnly at Ben. "You've got a pirate suit like Lewis, don't you?" he asked. "But yours is the real thing because you were a Johnny Depp stunt cat, weren't you?"

Lewis started bouncing up and down as George carried on talking.

"Ben was Superman's double, you know," George told Lewis. "And he will get his wings and save you, Lewis, if you fly off the trampoline because you're so skinny. Ben is not a cat. Ben's a stunt cat."

Lewis started laughing along with me as George told us his story, and even though he did not look at us, I could see he liked hearing us enjoying what he was saying.

"I will show Lewis how he is supposed to fight like Johnny Depp," he said for Ben. "George loves it when we fly so high we can touch the moon. Mum don't know we're pirates. But we do, don't we? We know that we are. George and me."

Chapter 10

The thing about being a single mum is that it's always one on one with your child. You're the only person in the world who lives with them day in, day out, the only one who completely understands their needs—and if your child is autistic there are a lot of those. Howard was a good dad to George: they went swimming or to the cinema together, he would look after George for a couple of hours if I needed him to and he'd spent our first Christmas in the new house with us. But we still didn't do the parenting together day to day, which meant I had no one to chat to about a bad day, leave in charge for a few minutes when it all got too much or have a good cry on. At least not until Ben came along.

Before he became part of the family, George and I were together every minute of every day when he wasn't at school and there were times when I'd wondered if I had the strength to answer another of his questions or the patience to listen to more chanting. If George got something into his head he couldn't get it out and on days like that he would follow me around like a shadow as words rushed out of him about whatever was on his mind. Food was one of the things he talked about a lot and time was another.

"When will I be eating my tea?" he'd ask as soon as he got in from school.

"In just over an hour," I'd tell him.

"What time is that?"

"Five o'clock."

"What will I have?"

"Egg and beans."

"How many eggs?"

"One."

"Not too crispy?"

"No, George. Just right."

"Will the yellow be runny or hard?"

"Hard around the edges and runny in the middle," I'd tell him, knowing that was the way he liked it.

"Will I have chips with one egg and beans?"

"If you like."

"Will the white be big?"

"Not too big."

Then George would think for a minute. "Stop!" he'd exclaim. "I want pasta and sauce."

"OK."

"Will it be the normal sauce?"

"Yes, George."

"No. I want chips and egg."

"OK."

If George ever stopped talking, it was only for a second before he began again.

"Mum, mum, mum, mum, mum," he'd chant as he followed me from room to room. "Mum, mum, mum, mum, mum."

"Yes, George?"

"I want egg and chips."

"OK."

"What time will I have it?"

"Five o'clock."

"How many hours is that?"

"It's one hour and twenty-nine minutes."

"How many minutes?"

"Eighty-nine."

"How many minutes and seconds?"

"Eighty-eight minutes and forty-five seconds."

"I didn't like my lunch today."

"Why not?"

"The yogurt was funny."

"Was it?"

"It was a different yogurt to what I like."

"I don't think it was, George."

"Yes it was."

I'd once given him a raspberry yogurt instead of a strawberry one and had never heard the end of it.

"My apple wasn't crunchy like yesterday's."

"Wasn't it?"

"My juice tasted different."

"Did it?"

"Warm."

Sometimes I'd try to walk away, but George wouldn't stop talking.

"The butter came out the side of my crackers. I don't ever want them again."

"You don't have to have them, then."

"I don't want them again."

"I know, George."

"I don't want crackers again."

"OK, George."

"I don't want crackers."

On and on it went, and if I tried telling George that I had a headache or had answered as many of his questions as I could for that day, it didn't make a difference.

"Mum is a bit tired," I'd say.

"Ryan breathed on me in school. He smelled of cheese and onion crisps."

"Did he?"

"Yes, and James pushed me."

"Did he?"

"In the hall. In the hall. In the hall. He has yellow in his ears. It makes me sick. I can't look."

He followed me everywhere: if I was in our tiny kitchen cooking, George would stand a foot away and I'd trip over him; when I went for a bath, he'd sit on the toilet; when I went to brush my teeth at night, he'd be right behind me. The only way to get him to leave me alone was by distracting him. Sometimes I'd suggest a game of hide and seek just so that I could lie under the duvet for a few minutes. As George ran around the house looking for me, I'd lie in the dark and wish it could swallow me up.

But just as Ben changed things for George, he changed them for me too. With him around, I started to get a few minutes' break as he played with George, which meant that I could nip off for a quick bath or go into the garden to quietly deadhead the roses. And as much as Ben understood what George needed, he also knew when I was at my lowest, which was usually at the end of a tiring day. When George finally fell asleep, I would sit with him to make sure he had really settled and Ben would jump on to my lap.

"Another long day, Baboo," I'd sigh as I stroked him and he'd look at me, starting to purr.

It's amazing what that sound did for me. It was like the rhythm of the sea or the rumbling of a train on its tracks, regular and soothing. Every mother worries if she's doing her best but it's hard when you're on your own and there's no one to talk to about all those doubts and fears. The thoughts would whizz around my head as I sat in George's bedroom with the low light of the lamp shining across his face and looked at him sleeping. But the sound of Ben's purring as I stroked him made me feel better. It was as constant as he was: day in, day out, he was a reassuring presence watching over us and sharing our laughter and troubles.

When I was finally sure George was going to sleep for a few hours at least, I'd go downstairs and look around at all the clearing up that had to be done, with Ben weaving in and out of my legs.

Sit down a minute, Julia. Have a quick rest. It will all still be there in half an hour.

So I'd sit down, give Ben a cuddle and feel a bit more of the tension disappear as I stroked him.

How are you? Are you OK? Have you got a bit more of a hug for me?

Just those few quiet minutes with Ben were often enough to calm me down. Instead of worrying about my health and George's, what was going to happen at school, whether he'd ever learn to let me hug him or say the words "I love you," I'd chat to Ben and it would all feel a bit less frightening. Call me batty but that's how it was.

The most important thing Ben gave me was his love for George. It was so strong that at first I had hardly been able to understand it; I'd even wondered if I was imagining the bond between the two of them to make myself feel better. I just couldn't understand how Ben seemed to know things— if George was quiet, he'd jump around to cheer him up and if George was over-excited, he'd lie quietly until he sat down beside him.

But slowly I learned not to question their bond. It was there and it was slowly opening up something deeper inside George, teaching him to love another living thing and care for it. Ben loved George just as much back too. As we sat on the sofa together while George was asleep upstairs, Ben would jump on to my lap, put his paws around my neck and give me the kind of cuddle I'd always longed for before looking up at me and purring.

George is a lovely boy, you know. I can see how kind he is, how well he plays with me. We have so much fun together.

Ben was two different, but very important, things to us: to George, he was the playmate who brought him out of himself; to me, he was the friend who reassured me that even on the most difficult days, things were just about OK.

George and I were in the car. It was a sunny day and we were driving to Cranford, a suburb just off the M4 motorway going out of London. It was only a couple of miles from

Heathrow, but even though it was so close to the airport, you could still get away from it all in Cranford because there was a huge park, where we'd gone all the time as kids. After turning off the main road, Dad would drive down a narrow lane until we got to a bridge over a stream, where he'd park the car.

"Right, then," he'd say to me, Tor, Nob and Boy as we sat in the back. "Let's see who catches the most, shall we?"

Then we'd get out of the car, troop down to the stream and spend the next few hours catching tadpoles before running round the woods playing cowboys and Indians while Dad and Mum lay on the grass. When we'd all had enough, they'd call us together to count the tadpoles before telling us to let them back into the stream.

I'd been doing the same thing with George for years: when the weather was good, as it was today, we got into the car and headed off to Cranford to find that little bit of the country hidden by all the concrete. Today, though, we had to drop off some shopping with Mum first and George stared out the window as we drove past Hounslow Heath.

"Ben used to ride the heath with Dick Turpin," he said in cat talk.

"Did he?" I asked.

"It was the most dangerous place in Britain, but Ben wasn't scared. Dick Turpin was. They went for miles in darkness on horseback."

George had never been able to get enough of the story of how Dick Turpin would ride across Hounslow Heath before stopping at the Bell pub so that he—and his horse—could have a drink.

"Ben and Dick Turpin were on the heath?" I asked.

"Yeah. They both had a gun." He stared out the window. "But the heath's been ruined now with a car park and rubbish. Most of the trees have been taken down and the traffic that drives around it gives the trees no good air, just fumes."

George was getting more and more aware of the environment as he got older and we talked about it often—how plastic bags hurt the birds and fishes who got caught in them, how we all need to be careful about litter to make sure we look after the nature around us—because George took everything in, so many facts and figures. As I pulled up outside Mum's house, he looked at the army barracks opposite.

"Ben wants me to be a soldier in the army when I'm eighteen," he said. "He thinks I'd be a good soldier. He was until he went to war, but it's not easy, you know, having to run with a gun and shoot people. He didn't shoot. He don't like shooting. He just made bang bang and they all run away."

"Where did they go?"

"He don't know. But he got shot in the arm and foot. It blew his boots off. He has a hole in his hat. He lost his best friend and they was young and now their family cries."

"Are they sad?"

"You have to march and polish your boots and sleep in a tent and drive fast away from bombs. You have to hide down holes in the ground. You can't join the army if you have ADHD. You can't join the army. I could because I don't have ADHD any more, do I, Mum?"

I looked at George, who turned his face away from me.

"You're much better now," I told him. "You're a good

boy."

He didn't say any more as he stared out the window, but I wanted to get back to our conversation, see if I could keep it going, because time had stopped as it always did now when we talked and lost ourselves together.

"Why did Ben leave the army?" I asked.

"He was musical and played the trumpet," George told me. "But he got hurt and he's not going back because they're bossy bossy."

George often repeated words like that—it was something he'd always done.

"He don't like jogging and he can't lay in at the weekends in the army," he said. "He's not stupid. He loves laying in."

"What did he do after the war?" I asked.

"He did work on the gate at the barracks," George told me, looking at the army buildings. "But someone called him Kitty Kitty and he didn't like it. His gun got heavy and he dropped it. It went off. Someone died but it was an accident. No crime, no murder. That's why Ben is at home right now." He stared at the barrack buildings.

"Salute the guard!" George suddenly shouted. "Salute the guards! March two, three, four, march two, three, four."

He started to chant over and over as I got out of the car to run into Mum's.

"Here's your shopping," I shouted to her.

"Want a cuppa?" Mum asked as she came to meet me.

"No! I've got to go. George is talking."

"What do you mean 'talking'?"

"I mean talking. Really talking. He's telling me about Ben."

I didn't stop to hear Mum's reply and I ran back to the car, where George was still chanting. I had to try to catch his attention again.

"I used to go to discos over at the barracks when I was young," I said loudly.

George stopped shouting. "I know," he said. "You was spoiled. Your name was bossy boots."

I laughed as I started up the car. "Look at that cat up in the tree," I said, pointing to an imaginary one that both George and I would see for real as we talked. "I hope he don't fall."

"He will. Ben knows him. He is always up the hospital. He falls out every week. He is a stupid climber. He likes his mum having to call the fire brigade out every week. He thinks he is a hero. He likes attention."

Soon we were turning into the narrow lane that led down to the stream at Cranford and the familiar road stretched in front of us.

"Granddad always said we had to beep the horn when we got to the bridge to let people know we was coming," I said in my cat voice. "And if someone beeped when we was fishing, we always got excited because we thought they was saying hello to us."

George didn't say anything as I slowed up to go over the bridge, but as I drove on to it, he suddenly sat up.

"Beep beep!" he cried. "We's coming. We can hear the fish under the bridge. Ben knows the fish. He comes over the bridge on his bike. But he always puts the fish back."

I could have laughed out loud now that George had started the conversation again. He really wanted to talk today.

"Does he?" I asked.

"Yes. Him and his friends meet up to fish. But he always catches the most. His great-uncle used to fish. The ducks come and watch him fish. They want his jam sandwiches. His friend has ham but the ducks want Ben's jam because they're vegetarian ducks."

We started laughing, both giggling our heads off as I parked the car.

"The fairies do live under the bridge," George told me. "They only come out when it's peaceful. The beep makes them jump. They can fly and they make bright lights. But you have to look hard to see their faces and wings. They laugh and giggle all the time. They love the sun. It makes them happy happy."

I wanted to grab George and squeeze him with pleasure. It was as though we were in our own world together and he was showing me the way into it. He was telling me a story about all the thoughts and pictures in his head—the fairies and soldiers, Ben's great-uncle and the vegetarian ducks—everything inside him so vivid and real.

I didn't want it to end.

"Does Ben have a rowing boat on the stream?" I asked.

"He does."

"And what does Ben do in the boat?"

"He has the fish jumping up to say hello as they pass. There's frogs and rats along the bank and they all look up to say hello. They love living here with no cars. It's all untouched and peaceful. Ben pulls over for lunch and shares his picnic basket."

"What does he have in it?"

"He don't travel light. He has the best big brown basket to open full of lovely foods. Jam, biscuits, prawn cocktail crisps, strawberry drink and ice cream. And a big flask of tea. He has a big red and white tablecloth. Just like Mum has."

"Does he?" I said, trying hard to keep my voice steady as emotion filled me.

"Yes," George said. "The sun is shining on the stream and he looks up at all the big weeping willows hanging low into the water. It's bumpy sometimes but he sings his heart out when he's floating down the stream. He can sing so loud through the woods it echoes. He sing sings while he goes down the stream nice and slow."

"What does he sing?"

" 'Why' by Anthony Newley."

"What did you say?"

" 'Why.' Your song."

I did not say a word. I'd always loved old crooners like Frank Sinatra, and "Why" by Anthony Newley was a song I'd sung a lot to George over the years, repeating the lyrics to him again and again, and hoping that on some level he would hear them and understand. But although I had sung it a thousand times, he had never shown me in any way that he did. I still loved those lyrics though because they told him all he needed to know:

I'll never let you go—why?—because I love you, [I'd
    sing to him]
I'll always love you so—why?—because you love me.

I looked at George and held my breath. "Ben sings 'Why'?" I asked quietly.

George got out of the car and walked over to the stream. I got out and stood beside him.

" 'Why,' " George said. "The song you have in the car. The song. "Because I love you.'"

It was the first time I'd ever heard him say those words, and the world seemed such a distant place as we stood together in that moment.

"That's right, darling," I told George. " 'Because I love you.' "

Chapter 11

George had been so determined to make his 11th birthday a double celebration for him and Ben that I'd had to buy him a fishing rod with a play mouse on the end. He'd decided that his big day was Ben's too after I'd told him that we didn't know when Ben had been born. We'd just had a tea party for the two of them in the garden. Mum, Boy and his children, Tor, Del and Nob, had all come over and George had insisted that I bought a chocolate birthday cake as well as a jam sponge because Ben liked both of them just as much. Now they were sitting on the lawn together and George picked up a can of string foam. He'd always loved it and every year on his birthday, I let him spray as much of it around the house as he wanted to, even though I always regretted it for days afterward as I kept finding bits all over the house. George's other favorite was party poppers, and we'd let off so many that the garden was covered in bits of multicolored paper.

"Are you ready and steady?" George said to Ben.

Ben rocked his head from side to side as George spoke and waited for the fun to start.

"Then go!" George shrieked and pressed the top of the can.

Pink string foam rushed out of the can and Ben made a run for it. But George was up and after him and string foam began flying around the garden as he sprayed wildly. Ben raced up on to the trampoline and George ran up to him. In seconds the trampoline disappeared under a mound of string foam. I could not stop laughing.

It made my heart sing to see the two of them together like this. Ben wanted to be a little boy so much that he'd recently even started climbing on to the pool table George had been given for Christmas, and whenever George took a shot, Ben would lie on a pocket before walking into the middle of the baize and batting a ball with his paw. He'd also decided that he wanted to go on the exercise treadmill I'd been given as a present because I couldn't leave George to go to a gym: when George walked on it, Ben took a stroll beside him. I giggled without stopping as I looked at them.

Ben was always finding new ways to get attention and his latest one was maybe the best. When he'd first come to live with us, I'd taken Ben back to the vet for check-ups, because I'd been warned that the cyst he'd had removed could mean he'd developed cancer, and when he came home George always made a fuss of him. When Ben had been given the all-clear, we'd all breathed a huge sigh of relief and he hadn't gone back to the vet until I'd noticed a lump behind his ear. The vet had diagnosed an abscess, which had to be lanced, and when Ben had come home stitched up and very quiet, George turned into Florence Nightingale for a whole week. Now I was sure that Ben was sometimes pretending to be under the weather just to get attention.

"He needs to rest," George would tell me seriously if Ben went quiet, and he would sit him down on the sofa with a pillow to lie his head on.

George didn't want Ben to be touched by anyone else if he thought he was ill and Ben was quite happy to be wrapped in blankets and cuddled for hours on end.

"Shall we watch a film?" George would ask him. "Would you prefer *Big* or *Garfield*? Or would you like a drink?"

Sometimes I'd catch Ben yawning, as if he was almost bored of the attention, but it usually took several days until George would begin to wonder if Ben might be having him on.

"Are you putting it on, Baboo?" he asked. "Are you really still sick?"

Each time he asked, Ben would give a pitiful miaow and George went straight back to loving him. It often took a few more days for Ben to finally get his fill of attention but when he did, he'd mysteriously wake up the next morning as right as rain.

Now I ran inside to get my camera as George and Ben played together. Running back out into the sunshine, I took a picture of the two of them together. I wanted to capture the smiles on both their faces forever—even though I knew there would be many more birthdays to celebrate together.

One of the questions George's psychiatrist asked him most often was about school.

"What do you think of big school?" she'd ask and George would usually refuse to say a word back to her.

Each time we left her office, George would tell me he hated his doctor but what he really hated were the questions she asked about big school because he knew it meant one thing—change. Moving from primary school to secondary school in September 2007, a few months after his 11th birthday, was going to be the biggest change he had ever known in his life and it frightened George, just as it frightened me.

I'd started talking about it all with the experts nearly two years before George was actually due to move, because it takes that long to get all the assessments done for a child with special needs. There are so many forms and reports that need to be done to make sure they get a place at the right school. Although it was clear that George couldn't go on to a mainstream secondary, because he'd struggled so much at primary, I still lay awake thinking about it night after night. How was he going to cope? George had found it hard enough to adjust when Miss Proctor had gone on maternity leave, so how was he going to react to a new place with new children?

The other thing that concerned me was this: as much as I knew George couldn't go to a mainstream secondary school, I was worried about sending him to a specialist one for children with learning difficulties. Until now, he had been with average children, and I could not help but worry that sending him to a specialist school would both label him as different forever and teach him new unusual behaviors. After all the progress he'd made I did not want George to go backward, and I wondered if sending him to a specialist school might only make things harder for him.

George picked up on all the meetings and discussions and got more and more anxious—chanting or talking endlessly to Ben about it all.

"I want to go to a normal school," he would say. "I'm not going to a special one. I'll get myself a book. I'll learn myself."

But although I understood how he felt, I knew that when push came to shove the best thing for George would be to go to a specialist school. So much had happened at his primary—the fights and misunderstandings, playground trouble and anger from parents who felt he was a bad influence—that it was impossible for George to feel settled and safe in that environment. I felt sure this was why he still hadn't learned to read or write properly, and although George was so good at maths that I could send him into shops with money from the age of five knowing he'd come out with the right change, it wasn't enough for him to cope with a mainstream school. The other problem was that George needed to be in a really contained environment, not a school where kids came and went, because he still had little sense of danger and had once even wandered out of school. I'd found him by pure luck when I was out in the car with Mum and saw a blond boy walking down a main road.

"Is that George?" I said.

"It can't be, Ju," Mum replied. "He's at school."

"Well, if it's not him then it's a boy who looks exactly like him."

I slowed down to get a better look. The boy was walking along the pavement with cars rushing on the road beside him and as I pulled up I could see that it really was George. My stomach turned over as I looked at him. He was out on a main road, among cars and people he didn't know or understand, when he should have been safe at school, and I felt angry that he'd been able to wander off.

"George?" I called out of the window.

He stared at me.

"What are you doing?"

"I'm going to the shop."

"I thought you were supposed to be in school."

He didn't say anything.

"I'm going to the shops, so why don't you get in with me?"

George got into the car and my heart hammered as I wondered how long he'd been out.

"When did you leave school?" I asked.

"I don't know."

But as the conversations went on about exactly which was the best school for George, I felt more and more confused. It's hard to know what's best when you've coped on your own for so long and then a stream of people start telling you what they think. On top of that, I'd had another run-in with the experts, which had knocked my confidence a bit. It had happened because George's sleeping problems had got so bad that he now got up in the middle of the night to do things, while asleep, and it wasn't just simple sleep-walking: he would take out his Legos and separate out the colors, or get a pack of cards and sort them all—still asleep but with his eyes open. He did it night after night, and it almost scared me when I saw him like that—like a ghost I couldn't talk to.

The doctors knew all about it and as George started his last year at primary school, they suggested that we visit a special center in central London, which helped children with sleeping and behavioral problems. I wasn't too keen, but I agreed to go and have a look, because I knew I had to try to keep an open mind. When we got there the center seemed nice enough. The building was big and airy, the kids had a pet rabbit and there was a lovely big art room full of brightly colored models stacked neatly on shelves. Then George and I were shown a room that had walls padded in blue and red and I was told it was the restraint room.

"When a child fights or punches we take them here," a man told me. "It's the best way to keep the children safe and contained until they calm down."

I thought of what George's psychiatrist had told me—that sometimes being a parent was about making a difficult choice for your child when it was best for them. But I wasn't sure this was the kind of thing she meant. Could I really allow George to be held down and put into a padded room? The thought of it made me feel sick. I knew the damage it would do. A few months before, George had told me that a teacher had locked him in a cupboard and although she said she hadn't, something had terrified him. George kept talking about the dark cupboard and the smell of paint, describing how he stood in the blackness and closed his eyes. I knew that he could interpret innocent incidents as threatening because he'd done so with me before. But when I looked at the restraint room, I knew that if he was held down and touched, however kindly or professionally, he would never recover from it.

After we were shown around the center, George and I went into a room to meet the people who worked there. Once again, they seemed as nice as all such people do, and they told us about what they did and how much they could help children like George. But as he sat in a chair and rocked, clicked his fingers and hummed, I could see the place scared him. I wasn't going to send him there. The psychiatrist was right: sometimes being a parent is about making really hard decisions and going against all the professional advice you're given if it feels wrong. It's all down to you and your child: what you know to be true and the instinct you have. I couldn't bear to cause George pain, even if some people thought it would help him in the long run, and as we left I told myself I'd find other ways of helping him. Now we had Ben I was sure I was going to keep finding them.

Anxiety was still one of George's biggest problems and even Ben hadn't rid him of it completely when it came to the outside world. George was happy at home but things were different when he left it, and as his physical tics like humming and tapping got worse, I could see for myself that he felt more and more under attack from the world around him. When George walked down the school corridor, the kids who brushed against him were bashing into him; when they came too close, they were trying to scare him; if they licked their lip, they were sticking their tongue out. So although I'd always made sure to take him out and about, I knew I had to do it even more now to stop him hiding.

So in the summer before George started secondary school, we went to even more places: to Bournemouth beach because he loved the sea or into town to Madame Tussauds or the London Aquarium. It wasn't plain sailing, because George didn't like all the people or eating when we were out. The one place we'd always been able to go was a nearby garden center with a café because the lady who ran it was kind enough to make toast just how George liked it—not too warm and served with gloves so that he knew no one had touched it. But now I learned to persuade him to eat when we were out by taking a packed lunch and making sure that no one came close enough to breathe on it; and if he got anxious when there was too much of a crowd, I would stand in front of him while he hid in a corner until the knot of people had passed by; or when he got angry because it had all got too much, I'd let him get it off his chest.

"I hate you," he'd scream again and again as he lay on the floor and I waited for him to calm down enough to get him back on to his feet. "Why did you make me come here?"

I knew I had to keep going to stop George building a shell around himself. But if dealing with him myself was one thing, other people's reactions were quite another. George looked like any other child at first glance and that meant strangers felt able to say whatever they liked when they thought he was being naughty.

"How can she let him get away with it?" I'd hear them say as he lay on the floor kicking and screaming. "It's disgusting."

"Parents these days. Don't know how to control their kids."

"Look at that boy. What kind of kid is he?"

Another day we were at an amusement park and got on a boat ride. George sat in his seat, looking as he always did when we were out—completely serious with a straight face and a tense jaw—and a man leaned toward him.

"Happy kid!" he said. "Don't look so miserable. It might never happen."

George didn't take a blind bit of notice, but I suffered the pain for him, feeling angry that people could be so judgmental. Why did they think it was OK to be so cruel about a 10-year-old boy?

I worried all the time that George was taking it in and hoped that some of the nice things we saw and did went in as well. When we got home after all those stares and sniggers, I'd tell George that I loved him again and again, as if to try to wash away any bad memories he might have kept. He didn't say anything back, but he'd bash into me when he walked past, which was his way of telling me that he'd heard.

The problem of school still had to be solved, though, and when Michael Schlesinger, George's educational psychologist, told me about three that he thought might be good for George, I decided to visit them to see for myself. The first was in south London and Mum came with me. The place was like Fort Knox—all locks and doors—and from the moment I stepped inside, I knew it wasn't where George would want to be. The teachers seemed very good and they obviously controlled the classes well. But when a boy wanted to hug me and started screaming when he was stopped, something just didn't feel right. I couldn't tell you exactly why I knew I didn't want George to go to that school, but I didn't. The second place I visited was just the same and I was beginning to wonder whether I'd ever find the right school for George when I went to visit the final one that Mr. Schlesinger had suggested—Marjorie Kinnan in Feltham, about 5 miles from home.

What can I say? The moment I walked in, I knew it was right for George. Marjorie Kinnan took kids with all sorts of learning difficulties, from the not so bad to the extreme. But it wasn't a sad kind of place at all; in fact, that was the last thing it was. The rooms were light, there was color everywhere and you could tell from the way the classrooms had been laid out that someone had thought about making kids with special needs feel comfortable. There was no huge echoing hall to scare them or rooms so small they'd feel trapped. Instead the school was divided into class-rooms and spaces just big enough for children to feel safe. There was a music room stuffed with equipment and a soft playroom filled with bean bags. The teachers were quiet and calm, and there was no restraining. It was lovely and there was happiness in the air, which was all I wanted for George. But although I wanted him to go to Marjorie Kinnan, he still had to be assessed by one of their staff to make sure he was suitable.

"There was a woman watching me today," he told me after a Marjorie Kinnan teacher had gone into his primary school to observe him.

I wasn't sure how much she could have found out about George, as he told me he'd pulled his jumper over his head and refused to show his face again after cottoning on to what was happening. So I decided to try to encourage him.

"She's not there to look at you," I said. "She's there to look at the out-of-control kids, not you."

A few days later I got the good news that the woman had been back to see George again and he'd been accepted at Marjorie Kinnan. My little white lie had done the trick.

Chapter 12

George was sitting in the bath and Ben lay in the sink, keeping watch over him just as he always did. As a wasp flew past, Ben tried to bat it with his paw but missed.

"You're out of control, you are," George told him. "And you've got learning needs. You can't talk to people. You don't like peoples. You is not a people's person. But you don't have to go to school, do you? You work in China."

Chatting to Ben was for George now what having a cuppa with Mum was for me—a way to make sense of things. One day Ben was the manager of a shop in Hounslow high street and the next he was working in Outer Mongolia. But throughout all George's imaginative talk, tiny bits of the information he was picking up at his new school were pouring out. He'd been talking to Ben a lot like this since starting at Marjorie Kinnan, because his first few months there had been hard and George needed to make sense of it all. Everything was new—buildings, faces, smells, voices, lights, toilets, even the height of the chairs at the desks—and with all those unfamiliar things to get to know it was no surprise that he'd found changing schools difficult.

At first, George's new class teacher, Miss Worgan, had told me that he was withdrawn and uncooperative. George had refused to look at her or do any work, sit still or answer questions, and although I knew this was all part of the process, it had worried me when I was told that he'd started copying behaviors he saw in the kids around him. George was doing things he had not done for a long time, like making sudden animal sounds to make his classmates laugh, and I knew I had to sort it out quickly or else it would just get worse.

"You have to stop copying and start showing who you really are," I told him. "You must show your teachers that you're sensible and kind because I know you are, and if you act sensibly the other kids will follow. I bet Miss Worgan would love to see the real you, not the naughty you, and I think Ben would like that too."

"Would he?"

"Of course. Ben knows what a good boy you are. He wants other people to see it too."

It was a step forward in itself that George and I could have conversations like this now. When George and I had started using cat talk, I'd sometimes wondered if I was doing the right thing encouraging it, because I did not want him to stop using his own voice. But as time had passed he was using cat talk less and speaking to me more in his own voice, which was how he told me some sad news when he came home from school. As the months had passed and his behavior had settled, George had made great friends with his learning support assistant, who was called Mrs. Ward, and although the only thing I knew about her at first was that she smelled of coffee—but then again most adults seemed to smell of coffee to George—he'd started telling me more. Mrs. Ward talked to him about everything from what she'd done over the weekend to where she went on holiday, and George had clicked with her because she spoke to him like a real person. So when Mrs. Ward told him that her dog had died, he was upset.

"Mrs. Ward is sad," George said when he got home from school.

"I'm sure she is. I'm sure Mrs. Ward loved her dog."

"She did. I wanted to tell her that her dog is in heaven."

"Well, you can tomorrow if you want to."

"No. No. You don't tell anybody."

"Why not?"

"You just don't."

George couldn't quite bring himself to say the words out loud, but just the fact that he'd wanted to say them was encouraging. And Mrs. Ward wasn't the only person he was showing concern for. The longer Ben was with us, the more George was getting well-known at Marjorie Kinnan for sticking up for his classmates. The kids there had problems of all kinds, physical disabilities as well as learning difficulties, and took the mickey out of each other as all children do. George had started to step in if he felt one was being particularly unfair to another.

"You need to take a look in the mirror at yourself," he told a girl who was taunting another.

Her mum complained about what George had said, but I was quietly happy that he was speaking out. Plain speaking had gotten him into enough trouble in the past; at least it was being put to better use now.

Miss Worgan, Mrs. Ward and all the other teachers at Marjorie Kinnan were the best thing that could have happened to George. They had endless time to talk to him, but all the practical things they did made just as much of a difference. George was given Blu-tack to hold in his hands to help him stop tapping them, which helped him concentrate; he had his own table, chair and drawer for school things, which solved his anxiety about people touching his things; he was allowed to change for sports lessons alone instead of in the changing room, which he'd always hated. The teachers even learned the fine art of being able to tell when George was really stressed and when he was just trying to push their buttons, which meant they could discipline or reassure him according to what he needed.

Each child at Marjorie Kinnan was treated as an individual and the patience everyone showed was getting real results: something had begun to click inside George when it came to learning and he was finally showing an interest in his lessons. It was happening very slowly, and I had to be careful not to ask him too many questions because he didn't want to talk about it too much. But after a day at Marjorie Kinnan, George went up to his bedroom when he got home and sat down with Ben. Then he'd get out a book and talk to Ben as he turned the pages, while Ben watched. Sometimes George would tell his own story to go with the pictures, but sometimes he would even try to read the book itself.

"Aaaannnnd," George would say, as he stared at a page.

Each word would be drawn out almost forever, but as I peered quietly around the door to watch him with Ben I'd feel full of hope.

The combination of Ben at home and a school that suited him so well were having a knock-on effect on other things too. George had started wanting to make decisions for Ben about when he should have food or when it was time for them to play, which I hoped would help him make more for himself; and talking to Ben was stopping him from bottling up his worries, which had made him calmer.

"Do you know we're going to run out of oil one day and then all the lights will go black?" George would tell Ben. "Do you know that swans get caught in plastic bags and die?"

As George talked, Ben would look at him very seriously, his bright eyes shining with interest in what his friend was telling him.

No, I didn't. That's awful, George. I don't like swans because they hiss if I get too close, but I still wouldn't want one to be hurt.

Another topic they went over regularly was the wars in Afghanistan and Iraq.

"There's a war," George would say to Ben. "And soldiers die. Bang bang. In the sand. People are killing each other. They need to stop. The guns need to be taken away like the cars. Guns kills people like cars kill the trees."

Or we'd be watching the news and George would see pictures of children orphaned by famine or disease.

"Look at the children," he'd say to Ben. "It's sad. Why is that happening? Mum says them people haven't even got fresh water." Then George would look at me. "Can't we give the children a home here, Mum?"

"I'm not sure we could fit all of them into our house," I'd tell him.

"But we should help them, shouldn't we?"

"I hope we can."

"So do I, Mum. Help the children children."

"Is that what you'd like, George?"

He looked at me as if I was completely mad. "Of course, Mum. It's good to help people. Don't you know that? I thought everyone knew that."

George could not stop laughing. I had gone out for an hour and Mum had been sitting with him, and he'd complained of a headache. So she'd gotten the sticky liquid medicine I gave George, because he couldn't swallow pills, but he had gotten the giggles as she tried to give him a spoonful. Just as Mum had gotten the medicine nearly into his mouth, George had moved and her hand had slipped. As usual, Ben was sitting below them, watching what was happening, and now his back was matted with sugary medicine and I was chasing him around the kitchen trying to get it off with a wet cloth.

"At least he won't get a headache," George shrieked.

I didn't have time for this. We were having a Halloween party, a really big one, and people were going to start arriving soon. George was dressed up as a devil in a red cape and horns with a face to match, I was a dead bride and Ben? Well, Ben wore a dinner suit every day, thanks to his white nose and chest, so he didn't need to dress up. As I made a grab for him, he ran off again and I wondered if he thought I was just playing with him—or whether he knew he was playing with me.

There was still so much to do because this was going to be a party that everyone would remember. I'd had big ideas about how I was going to celebrate the Halloween of 2008. I'd had a small do the year before with family and it had gone so well that this time I wanted to do something even better. I'd been thinking back to the gardening and games nights on the estate and had decided that lots of people we knew should get involved.

I've always loved a get-together—from the birthday parties I had as a kid, when Mum would buy me a lovely dress and invite all my friends over for Coke floats, to the bashes Michelle and I had with our neighbors and the kids when we'd dance to Dolly Parton as she wanted, or Elvis as I did, and all the children would plead for something a bit more up-to-date. I like everything that a party involves, from buying food and decorating to getting dressed up and dragging out all the old CDs, because when the house fills up with people and I hear the sound of them laughing, I know there's nothing better in the world than everyone enjoying themselves. Life's so full of trouble that we all need those times when we let our hair down and just have fun, don't we?

George wasn't so sure, though, when I told him what I wanted to do.

"Why don't you invite some friends from school?" I said. "It'll be fun."

"I don't want to."

"Go on, George."

"No."

"I'll make sure Lewis dances for you."

If anything was going to persuade him, that would. Over

the years, George had had to get used to parties because our family got together at any chance. But George had a mixed relationship with our celebrations. Although he loved getting ready for them, decorating and planning what we were going to do, as the party started he'd usually go to his bedroom or stand on the sidelines, unsure of what to do with all the people and noise. Lewis's dancing, though, was the one thing George always loved watching, and he wanted everyone else to like it as much as he did.

"Turn the music down," George would shout when he'd decided it was time for Lewis to show us his moves. "Everyone move back. Lewis is the best dancer there is. He can dance just like Michael Jackson. He loves Michael Jackson. I do too."

Then when he was sure that everyone was gathered in a proper circle, George would hit the button on the stereo and Lewis would start dancing. He could zombie walk to "Thriller" like the King of Pop himself and George would tap his foot to the music as he watched everyone looking at Lewis.

"Did you see Tor clapping her hands to Lewis's dancing?" he'd ask me afterward. "Boy said 'Woo' when he finished, which means he must have liked it too because that's what people say when they like something."

Lewis danced at every party and even if George then went back to stand in the corner and wave people away when they got too close, I was glad he had a way of being at the center of things for a few minutes. A lot of parents with children like George might not throw parties because they think it would be too much. But just as learning to say please was important for George to learn, so was understanding that fun was a part of life. I'd always believed George would learn things by seeing them, and getting as comfortable as he could among people was one of the lessons I wanted to teach him.

Now you should know by now that I don't do things by halves and this Halloween party was no different. Neighbors and friends had been invited, and Mum was standing in the kitchen dressed as a dead pensioner while I chased Ben around. Nob, Tor and her husband Del, Boy, Sandra and the kids were all coming. Arthur, who'd moved away from the estate with his mum a few months before, so we didn't see so much of him, was also invited and the guests of honor were going to be five of George's classmates. I knew that just like him they'd never get to go trick or treating or be invited to the kind of parties that most kids go to, so I wanted to give them a Halloween memory to keep forever.

Once I'd decided to do that, what happened next was what usually happens with me: I didn't know when to stop. I'd done an extreme makeover on the whole of the downstairs of the house, but instead of making it look better, I had transformed it into a creepy haunted house. I wanted people to feel as though they were in another world from the moment they stepped on to our driveway. After searching the Internet for ideas, I'd come across a Web site run by a man in America who sold everything you could think of for Halloween, and while I knew they went to town over there, this was something else. The man had fake dead bodies hanging off the front of his house and had even built his own coffins. It was amazing. Even though I was going to have to do something on a smaller scale, because there was only so much in the budget after all, there was one thing he had that I wanted.

The man made and sold "butlers"—six-foot lifelike figures that looked a bit like Herman off *The Addams Family* and came dressed in suits, with rigid hands to hold a tray and a recorded voice like the ones some dolls have, only the butlers' voices sounded not cute but scary. Those butlers were so brilliant I knew I had to have something like them, and to do them proud I was going to have to make everything else just as good. Getting the butlers shipped over was going to be way too expensive, though, so I tracked two down on a Web site closer to home, ordered them and set about creating props.

The first thing I made was gravestones out of polystyrene blocks that I'd painted gray, before twisting chicken wire into body shapes and dressing them in ripped clothes to create fake dead people. Their heads were made out of witches' masks stuffed with wet newspaper, and I'd bought bales of hay that were now on the driveway with pumpkins perched on them. The dead bodies were hanging off the front of the house, along with two gray skeletons, broomsticks and spiders, and I'd even gotten a smoke machine so that when people arrived, they had to walk through the foggy graveyard past a fake guillotine, where I was going to take photos of the partygoers. The cost had gone up and up, of course, but my family had helped once again because they're good like that and always join in my schemes.

Earlier in the day, Mum had come over to decorate the lounge and we'd hung cobwebs, spiders and bats all over the walls. Then we'd put huge pumpkin lampshades over the lights to make the room glow orange and I'd rigged up a strobe light to make sure things looked really creepy.

George had had a face like thunder when he got home from school and saw what we were doing.

"She's not right, is she?" he said to Mum as he pointed at me. "Who'd do all this? This is too much."

"I know, love," she replied. "But that's your mum and she's been like it since she was a little girl. She's a dreamer."

George was right in a way. I'd gotten so carried away that I'd even continued the party out into the back garden with another fake graveyard on the lawn and a haunted house in the shed with lucky-dip buckets full of sawdust, baked beans and mud. But I was determined to make sure that George and his friends had the night of their lives and I was hoping that even if he did not like it now, George might get a bit more interested when the party started.

Nerves filled me, though, as the house filled up and all George's classmates arrived, and friends, family and neighbors too. Everyone looked fantastic: Lewis was a pirate of the Caribbean, Wendy, Kayleigh and Sandra had come as witches, Tor was a ghost, Boy was covered in chains and Nob wore his jeans because he'd wanted to come as Michael Myers from the *Halloween* film but we'd all decided that he might scare the kids too much.

George was quiet at first, despite the fact that from the moment people started arriving, Ben had been rushing around as though it was his very own party. He weaved in and out of people's legs, skittered across the graveyard and dived into the lucky-dip buckets. But as George watched Ben having such a good time, he slowly joined in himself. Soon he was eating sweets and hot dogs with his friends, jigging to the music a bit and even visiting the graves. One of his classmates got so excited by the whole thing that he ended up hitting me over and over with his toy sword, which made George roar with laughter.

The party just kept getting bigger: kids who were out trick or treating dropped in to get some sweets, and the house ended up heaving so much that even the police turned up. They weren't there to arrest anyone: they'd heard about what we were doing from a neighbor who'd seen me getting it all ready and they'd brought a bucket of sweets and a photographer from the local newspaper to take a picture of the kids. We had a great old time as the bobbies tucked into hot dogs and the pensioners from the bungalows came for a look with their grandkids. Everyone was welcome, and of course the night ended with Lewis dancing to "Thriller."

I was just so pleased that George had joined in and although he didn't say much about it at first, he came home the next week and told me that his school friends had been talking about the party.

"Miss Worgan said it sounded fantastic," George said. "We're going to talk about it in assembly."

"Are you?"

"Yeah."

"You could tell them how I made fake graves and you wore a red cape."

George looked thoughtfully at me. "Will we do it again next year?"

"Yes. Even bigger."

Ben, sitting on George's lap, meowed and I looked at him. He had loved the party and even though George didn't say any more, I was beginning to think that he might just have enjoyed it too.

After that day at Cranford, George had started to mention love in a roundabout way. Sometimes when I tried telling him not to do something naughty, he'd grin as I spoke.

"You know Ben loves you, don't you, Mum?" George would say as he laughed. "He do or he don't? He does or he don't? He would or he wouldn't? I'm going to ask him."

Or I'd be on the phone to Mum and he'd suddenly shout down the stairs.

"I love you, Nan!"

"Did you hear that?" I'd ask Mum excitedly.

He did not say the words "I love you" to any of us face to face, but that didn't matter. Just hearing George use the word "love" was more than I had ever thought was possible, and he showed there was so much more bubbling up inside him each time he hugged and kissed, petted and stroked Ben. But although he could show his affection to Ben, George still couldn't bring himself to do the same with me, so I held on to the times when we rough played together, as I had done since he was small. As he wrestled me to the floor, pushed his face close to mine or held me down as he pretended we were fighting, I was glad that he felt comfortable enough to do this with me. All boys enjoy tumbling around and I'd seen my brothers do it often enough when they were young, so I rough played with George because he didn't have a dad at home or brothers to do it with. I wanted him to have just a bit of time to feel free without do's and dont's, because there were a lot of those at home and school.

Rough play was George's way of getting close to me, so I'd laugh along as he bashed into me—even if it was a bit hard at times—enjoying the moment until he felt he'd got too close and pulled away as he told me I smelled or had funny hair. That always happened—George's senses got overloaded with information and he pulled back. But then he was showed his affection for me by rough playing and I loved it.

His other favorite game was to pretend to be a cat just like Ben, and he did it so much that I'd almost stopped noticing it by now. Getting down on the floor, George would crawl around with Ben or make purring noises like him. But when he started bumping into my legs or sitting closer to me on the sofa as he pretended to be a cat, I realized something was beginning to change. George still wouldn't even let me take his hand, but it was as if he was slowly trying to come physically nearer to me.

I was careful not to react, even though the longing inside me to hug and cuddle him was as strong as it always had been. Although I'd learned to push it down over the years, there were still moments when I saw other mothers pull their child on to their laps to give them a kiss or cuddle and felt a twist deep down that I'd never known that kind of love with George. So maybe that's why when he touched me for the first time, I almost didn't let myself think about it too much. It was as if I was scared to admit what was happening, in case he never came near me again.

It was a night like any other. I was on the sofa and George was sitting at the other end with Ben stretched out across his chest and shoulder as he ran his fingers through his fur. After a long cuddle, Ben jumped off George's lap and walked to the door into the garden to let us know he wanted to go out, and I got up to open it before lying back down on the sofa as George played on the floor. But when I settled back down George started to crawl over to the sofa. I didn't take much notice until I realized that he was about to climb up on to it. Without a word, George got up next to me and lay on top of me, stretching out his whole body against me just as Ben had lain on him a minute ago. I could hardly believe it was happening.

George softly rubbed his face against mine and I didn't move a muscle, afraid of making a wrong move and scaring him. I had never been so close to him. I felt his weight against me and I didn't want to ruin this precious moment.

"Ben was a Japanese sumo wrestler," George said.

"Was he really?"

"Yes. He does karate and kickboxing. He is a black belt, I know. He won the world's best karate cat but didn't want the trophy because he's not a cat."

I wasn't sure what to do. I lifted my hand and gently pushed my fingers through George's hair as he lay against me. If I cuddled him just as he'd cuddled Ben, maybe he'd be comfortable.

"You've got a hairy face," George said and I stopped moving my hand for a moment, thinking that he was about to draw away.

But he didn't. Instead George carried on lying on me and I stayed completely still, willing myself not to scare him away. He was so close I could feel his breath as it danced on my cheek.

"Don't move your hair on me," George said. "I don't like your hair."

"I won't."

"Don't stare at me. I don't like it."

"I won't."

I lowered my eyes as I pushed my fingers into George's hair again and ruffled it back from his forehead. Just to be this close to him was something I had imagined so many times. Could I allow myself to accept it was real now that it was actually happening?

"Ben thinks Buster doesn't have manners," he said and I smiled as I thought of the tabby imposter that Ben still didn't like at all. "But Buster don't have manners because he lives on the streets and Ben forgets he was homeless once and used to eat crisps out of the bin."

I giggled and lifted my head to look at George. I couldn't stop myself. But this time he was looking back at me with his eyes so blue and clear.

"Ben has traveled the world so he can help other cats," he said.

"Where has he been?"

"He went to Cyprus on holiday."

I flexed my fingers and scratched them softly across George's scalp. His hair was so soft, his body so relaxed as he cuddled into me. "Was it hot in Cyprus when Ben was there?" I asked him.

"Yes. The cats stay by the pool all day because it's hot. Ben wears factor 50."

I curled my hand around George's ear before rubbing his nose softly, careful not to be too greedy to touch him, until he suddenly sat up.

"I'll go and find Ben," he said, lifting himself off me and walking toward the door.

"OK, George," I said as he disappeared into the garden.

I stayed quite still, my breath stopped inside me. To hug my child, feel the weight of him after 11 years of empty arms, was a gift I'd never dared hope to be given.

Chapter 13

Halloween was such a success that the local housing association heard about it and contacted me to ask if I'd be interested in volunteering for them. They said they wanted to train me for a qualification that would allow me to organize community events and eventually get paid for doing it. I was so pleased that I filled out the forms they gave me listing all the reasons why they should give Julia Romp a chance at working. Then I went to a meeting in a room full of people wearing suits and panicked. Who was I kidding? Organizing things to help people get out and about in their community might be the best kind of job I could think of, but it wasn't my world. I had had three jobs ever since George was born—a day shift, an evening one and the nighttime one, all with him—and I couldn't juggle all that with work outside my home.

The next Halloween was a whole year away, though, and that seemed far too long to wait for another party. I was itching to get organizing again, and then fate played its hand, just as it often does, when I got a letter from Marjorie Kinnan. The school wanted parents to do things for Christmas to help raise money for a new minibus, and that was all the excuse I needed. My mind went into overdrive as I thought about what I could do. A carol concert? No. As Mum said, I was tone deaf. An ice rink? No. That was a step too far, even for me. Then I had the perfect idea: a winter wonderland, a Christmas scene conjured up at our house in west London that would make people think they'd flown to Lapland for an audience with Father Christmas himself. There would be lights and music, reindeer and snow. Loads of people on the estate didn't have the money to take their kids to see a Father Christmas in a shopping center because it cost a bomb, but maybe I could raise a bit for Marjorie Kinnan by creating something on their doorstep and asking them to give what they could. Whatever we raised would be a bonus, because at the very least people from around the estate could have a festive night out with their kids and I wanted to do something, however small, to thank Marjorie Kinnan for all they had done for George. The winter wonderland would run through the whole of December to give people the chance to come back again and again if they wanted to.

I've always loved Christmas. When we were young, Dad would stand at the bottom of the stairs and I'd feel my heart racing as I waited for him to call us downstairs. The moment he did, Nob, Tor, Boy and I would tumble down, tripping over each other to get to the present pile first. Then as I grew up I learned to love Christmas even more, because I got to make it last for weeks as I decorated and shopped, wrapped presents and sent cards.

But for George Christmas was both a happy and difficult time. It was happy because he liked all the build-up and
loved to decorate the house just as much as I did. We had
great fun decking out the place and George had built up a
huge collection of singing Christmas toys over the years
that always took pride of place. He had everything from a
reindeer and a snowman that sang to three cuddly mice
dressed in Christmas gear and a penguin in a Santa suit
which could also hold a tune. It was chaos when he switched
them all on, but George loved those toys and I loved seeing
his face as they made a racket. The difficult bit always came
on Christmas Day itself, because George never reacted to
the expectation hanging in the air. It made him feel uncomfortable—so much pressure on one day when he wanted
every one to be pretty much identical. So over the years I'd
learned not to make too much of Christmas Day and treat it
like any other. George had presents and sometimes he'd
open them; more often he didn't. I had a wardrobe full of
wrapped boxes that I'd collected over the years.

As I thought about my winter wonderland, I wondered
how George would react to it. I knew he'd enjoyed
Hallowe'en but the party had been pretty much full of
people he knew and the winter wonderland would mean a
lot of strangers coming to the house. It would be hard for
George, but after thinking about it a lot, I decided to give it
a go. I so wanted to do it and George could take part or not
as much as he wanted to. If it was too much for him, I'd
make sure no one went into the house so that he could have
it all to himself with Ben.

The more I thought about the winter wonderland, the
more I had a picture in my head. Just as I'd done for

Halloween, I was going to make a little world for people to lose themselves in. Night after night, I stayed up planning it all, pictures whirling around inside me as I dreamed. When it was all finally clear in my head, I got to work. The first thing I had to organize was the lights, because they're the Mick Jagger of Christmas—the bit that gives it rock, roll and sparkle. Lots of people decorate the outside of their houses with lights for Christmas—fairy lights, flashing Santas, glowing reindeers and stars twinkling in the darkness—and I loved seeing houses done up like that. It's like a Christmas card you give to everyone who walks past your front door.

I'd been decorating our house with lights ever since we moved, but that wouldn't be nearly enough for the winter wonderland. Our little driveway was going to have to be transformed into a festive scene to draw people in and a few fairy lights just wouldn't do. So the first job was to track down lights—stars and bells, a Christmas tree and train, lights to go in trees and all over the front of the house—and even though my budget was small, it's amazing what you can find on eBay. I'd also decided to line the drive with Christmas trees strung with fairy lights to make a proper entrance. I didn't even let myself think about the electricity bill; I was far too carried away to worry about it.

The wonderland also needed to have a centerpiece and I wanted it to be a sleigh. So I jumped at the chance when my friend Sarah said her lovely dad, Simon, who was a woodworker, could help me. I sketched him a picture of my dream machine, which was big enough to fit a dozen people, but I went back to the drawing board after finding out that the wood alone was going to cost me £500. This was Hounslow, after all, not Harrods. In the end Simon made me a sleigh that was big enough to fit a couple of kids in, so they could have a photo taken, and he didn't charge me a penny for his time because he was so kind. He did such a brilliant job that when I finally went to pick up the sleigh, I had to have a sit in it before rushing home so that Mum and I could paint the wood cherry red and gold.

The sleigh had to be drawn by reindeer, of course, and once again I was inventive. After buying reindeers, or rather reindeer shapes made out of chicken wire and covered in fairy lights, I stitched each one a jacket, hat and scarf to wear so that they looked a bit more realistic. Then I scattered hay around their feet and put two buckets beside the reindeers—one filled with hay so that the kids could feed them and the other with sand, which would be Santa's magic dust to wake up the reindeers when he needed to go off delivering presents.

The final thing I wanted was a post box, because kids can't help but get excited by posting a letter to Santa full of all their Christmas wishes. It couldn't be one of those plastic toy post boxes, because the kids would know that Santa would have a much better one than that. So I got on to Google and found a man in Dorset who made them out of empty gas canisters, which he painted to make look like the real thing. I swear that post box looked like one of Her Majesty's own when it arrived. After that there was just the fancy dress left to buy. I was going to take pictures of all the kids who came so that they could have a memento of their visit and I wanted them dressed up as snowmen, elves and snow princesses. There would also be a Father Christmas outfit for the dads to put on if they wanted to and a Christmas cape for pets who felt like joining in.

It was all hands on deck in the days leading up to the grand opening. Mum, Nob, Tor and Boy all helped rig up the lights and Wendy and Keith came over too. Ben scampered around our feet, clawing up the Christmas trees and getting tangled in lights. The moment I unveiled the sleigh, he jumped straight in and had to be lifted off to make sure he didn't leave scratch marks on the paintwork. He meowed angrily as he was put on to the cold ground and his fun was ruined.

Can't I have another go on the sleigh? It's Christmas! I want to have fun!

George was a bit put out by everything that was going on.

"All those kids will break the sleigh," he kept telling me. "I don't want them coming here."

"It's for your school," I said, to try to reassure him. "Just think of all the fun you'll have on trips in the minibus when the school buys it, and we will be raising money to help do that. If you don't want to see all the people, you don't have to. You can stay nice and warm inside with Ben and he'll look after you."

I just hoped that George would get a bit more comfortable with our winter wonderland when he saw everything finished. The Christmas lights might help when they were switched on but if not, I'd have to roll out the big guns and get Lewis out on the driveway every night doing his "Thriller" routine.

A few days later, when everything was finally done, I walked out on to the drive with Mum. George was a few steps behind us and Ben was sitting in a tree watching as my hand hovered over a plug. With one final click the Christmas lights would go on and the winter wonderland would be open.

"Three, two, one," Mum said with a smile and I pushed the switch.

The house lit up like a Christmas tree. Red and green, white and blue lights—so many that for a moment I worried whether planes flying overhead to Heathrow might mistake my drive for a runway.

"It's so bright," George said with a gasp as he stared upwards.

Ben stared too as he peeped out from behind the branches.

It's amazing! Beautiful! When is Santa going to arrive? I can't wait to see him.

Ben raced down the tree, ran up to us and started weaving in and out of our legs like an eel. He miaowed again and again as we stared around us and I could understand how excited he felt by it all. This was it, the beginning of our Christmas, and everything was perfect. I'd even bought a snow machine for the final finishing touch because it wouldn't have been a proper winter wonderland without a few flakes puffing around.

I looked around at what we'd created and decided that if this didn't raise a good bit for Marjorie Kinnan I'd eat Santa's hat and Rudolf's too.

"I'm going inside," George said.

Ben ran into the house after him and I wished the two of them had stayed outside just a bit longer with Mum and me. I so wanted George to enjoy this.

"He'll be fine, Ju," Mum said as I went to fluff up the hay in the reindeer's bucket.

I looked around. It was 4:30 p.m. and the sky was black. Stars were twinkling overhead and I could see my breath puffing in a white cloud in front of me. I'd put up posters all over the area telling people that we were opening, but I wasn't sure how many were going to turn up.

"Shall I make some tea?" I asked Mum as we walked inside.

The next two hours dragged by as I kept refilling the pot and waiting for a knock on the door. Had I gone too far this time? Would people think I was completely round the twist? It was one thing to arrange a bit of apple bobbing and a game of rounders, but would people really turn up to all this?

Wendy's daughter Kayleigh was with us as we nervously waited to see if anyone was going to arrive. She had gotten so excited by all the work we'd been doing that she'd asked to help out. So I'd dressed her up in an elf suit and she was ready to go. Kayleigh was going to get the kids in and out of the sleigh so that I could concentrate on taking photos of them, and I'd asked George to hand out the fancy-dress costumes.

As Mum chatted about anything other than the winter wonderland, I could hear George laughing. I walked into the lounge to find Ben flipping around on the carpet. We'd bought him a cat-sized elf jacket and he was now pulling it off in disgust, wriggling like a worm as he tried to get out of it.

"He don't want to dress up," George said. As he lifted up Ben to help him out of the costume, I heard a ring on the doorbell.

"I don't like this," George muttered. "I don't like these people."

My heart felt a bit heavier than it should have done as I opened the door to find a woman on the doorstep with two little girls.

"I've seen a leaflet," she said. "Is it all right to visit?"

"Of course! Let me just get the bucket of sweets."

I grabbed it and walked outside with Mum and Kayleigh. The two little girls' eyes were out on stalks as they stared around.

"Would you like a photo on Santa's sleigh?" I asked them.

"Yes please."

"Well, then, you've got to dress up," I said and with that we were off. The winter wonderland was open for business.

Some nights there were only a couple of knocks on the door but on others we had a queue outside as though it was the first day of the sales. The doorbell usually started ringing around 4:30 p.m. after school had finished for the day and went on until about 9:30 p.m. Kayleigh was with me every night with her elf outfit on, ready to stand for hours in the cold because she was just like me—a dreamer who looked out into the wonderland and saw real reindeer stamping their hooves as Father Christmas himself stood beside the sleigh. Our winter wonderland wasn't made out of lights and plastic: to Kayleigh it was alive, and I hoped other children could feel the magic as we did.

"What are those?" kids would ask excitedly as they walked up the driveway and saw the buckets standing next to the reindeer.

"One has hay in it because the reindeer are always hungry and the other is full of magic dust so that Santa can wake them up when he wants to," Kayleigh would tell them proudly.

Mum also came to help us a lot of evenings, but George kept himself to himself in the house; even Ben running in and outside for a look didn't persuade him out. I didn't put any pressure on him as I welcomed people and took photo after photo of them to make sure I got a nice one. I just left George to it, because I knew that the only way he'd join in would be if he decided to himself—just as on the night of the Halloween party. So I looked after the winter wonderland with Kayleigh each evening and then after turning off the lights when everyone had finally gone home, I'd go inside and print out the photos I'd taken of our visitors and stick each one into a Christmas card ready for them to collect the next day. When that was done it was time to empty the post box. I answered all the kids' letters to Santa and made sure to tell each child that Father Christmas would try his hardest to get something from their wish list without promising them the earth.

For days George refused to come outside and I began to wonder if he ever would. He watched everything going on from the kitchen window because he couldn't get enough of the Christmas lights. But although he'd started coming to the door when there was a ring on it and would get me the sweet bucket to take outside, he did not want to come out himself. Maybe it was all too much. Maybe I was hoping for something that was beyond George, however much he had improved. But I should have trusted that Ben would be the one to find a way to persuade George outside, and even I could not get angry when he used his favorite enemy, the dog, to do it.

When a man arrived with a couple of yellow Labradors Ben went wild. First he ran in and out of the man's legs as the dogs stared at him from the end of their leads; then he jumped into the sleigh to show them who was boss before they got a chance to get on to it. When Ben darted around them, trying to make them bark, the dogs looked as bewildered as Jedi had been once. Suddenly they couldn't take it any more and started roaring at Ben, who danced away with a gleam in his eyes. I saw George at the kitchen window with tears of laughter running down his face.

"You're going to have to go inside before you cause too much trouble," I told Ben sternly and carried him into the house.

It didn't do any good, because Ben just sat on the windowsill with George behind him and screeched so loud that I thought he might drown out the Christmas music. As soon as the Labradors had gone, I went to get him back outside and George just couldn't resist following to see what else Ben was going to get up to.

"It would be so good if you could show the little ones what to do," I said to George as he stood on the doorstep, looking outside. "They're not sure about the fancy-dress costumes, so you and Ben could help them."

Ben sat just outside the door and looked at George.

Please come and play with me, George. Won't you come outside? It will be so much fun.

George hesitated for just a second before stepping out into the night. Ben came up to him and purred with excitement. He was almost beside himself, because he knew nothing could touch him now and he looked at me in triumph.

I'm George's cat. And he won't tell me off. He'll laugh when he sees me getting the dogs all excited.

"Why don't you have a look at the fancy dress and make sure it's all ready?" I said to George as he looked around.

He walked up to the box and started pulling things out while Ben jumped on the sleigh.

"He wants to be in a photo shoot," I said with a giggle.

"He do and he don't," George told me as he rooted through the box. "He was an actor once in Hollywood so he's good at photos and the sleigh might take off with him in it. He wants to visit Father Christmas."

After that, George started coming out every night, and the best time was having the winter wonderland all to ourselves as we got it ready each evening. George, Ben and I were in our own magical world as we sat on the sleigh telling stories or stood side by side staring up at the lights. I knew George felt at ease in this wonderland full of color because we had made it ours, which helped him cope when strangers came into it. George had his own way of dealing with them, of course: he would sigh if a child knocked the hay bucket over before telling me not to worry. Having lifted up the hay bucket and set it straight, he'd walk back to stand in front of the fancy-dress box and look just past the kids standing in front of him waiting to be given something.

"You can have this one," he'd tell one and hand over a reindeer suit.

"And you can have this," he'd say to another.

If their mums gave George a quick look, I didn't care.

People coming to our winter wonderland had to accept George for who he was, just as we accepted anyone who came.

"Come back tomorrow and bring your nan," he'd call when children left, before turning to talk to me. "We'll have them back, I think, because they can't go to the big shops, Mum."

"No, George," I told him and I'd feel warm even in the icy cold of a December night.

George took it all in his stride and I felt so proud of him. He didn't bat an eyelid about who came, and that was good because we had all sorts visiting. There was the woman with five children who used the filthiest language I'd ever heard in front of them but gave me a big thank-you when she left. Then there was the drunk dad who almost scared me when he turned up with his kids because everyone knew of him on the estate, but turned out to be so nice he gave me a fiver for the collection. People had just as many surprises in them on our new estate as they had had on the old one, and I was just happy to watch George and Ben together, standing side by side next to the fancy-dress box or watching over the sweet bucket.

"Just one packet," George would tell kids if they tried to grab a handful and then he'd give Ben an exasperated look.

What can you do, George? Some kids are just like that, aren't they? But it's Christmas and they're having fun, so we'll ignore it.

As Christmas got nearer and nearer Ben led the way. He sniffed at people as they got on the sleigh, ran up and down the Christmas trees lining the drive and jumped into the fancy-dress box. In fact, he seemed to think he was in charge of Christmas now. George was a bit more hesitant, but he wasn't the only one who found it hard to be around all those people and their noise. One busy night, a neighbor turned up with his grandkids, who were visiting from Ireland, and they all started trying to pile on to the sleigh for a picture—all except one of his granddaughters, aged about seven, who hung back. I could see that everyone was making too much of a scene for her as they tried to get her into a costume.

"If you want her in one so much, why don't you put one on?" I told her granddad.

"Get the suit out, love," he roared with a laugh.

When he was all tuckered up as Father Christmas, the granddad got on to the sleigh and sat back with his wife beside him as his grandchildren hung off the sleigh around them. But the little girl still stood quietly to the side.

I bent down to her. "Don't worry about going on the sleigh," I said. "Why don't you feed the reindeer instead?"

As she went to fill up their bowls with hay, I took pictures of the rest of the family; I must have taken 30 before I got the right one. Then the family went off home.

The next day the granddad came back and this time he had just the little girl with him.

"She wants to have her picture taken," he told me and she climbed into the sleigh.

There she sat with her beautiful face and curly hair, dressed up as a snow princess and I captured the moment on film. Now she felt comfortable enough to smile.

Sadly, though, not everyone was quite so happy about what we were doing. A few days after the winter wonderland began, I opened the door to find a woman standing outside.

"I'm from the housing association," she said. "We've had a complaint that your lights are too bright."

I'd wondered if she was joking. What kind of Scrooge was going to try to ruin Christmas for everyone? But the woman explained that she had to investigate the complaint because they'd had a phone call. I didn't understand why one bad apple would try to ruin life for all the good ones, but even though I didn't know who was giving the Grinch a run for his money, I was pretty sure that all they really wanted to do was make trouble.

So I explained to the woman from the housing association about what George, Ben and I were doing and she listened to what I had to say. There was just one bit of official business to sort out: when I told the woman I was taking photos of kids, she said she'd have to check with her manager that it was OK to do that on property owned by the housing association. The message came back that I could snap away as long as the kids had an adult with them. I was glad to see a bit of common sense.

"It's a good thing for the community," the woman said when she rang up, and the housing association even put a check for £100 in the post for the collection.

The money was brilliant but what really made all my Christmases come at once was watching George outside with Ben, interacting with strangers and getting involved. After all the years of taking him out and George finding it so difficult to be among people, he was finally doing it. He and Ben were like Butch Cassidy and the Sundance Kid: a perfect pair.

I was not going to let myself get upset. I had been going to Christmas concerts for years and I couldn't believe that I was still harping on about this one thing that I wanted and which never happened. During all his years at primary school, I'd gone to every one of George's concerts and watched as his classmates came on stage and stared out into the audience, searching for their mum or dad to give them a reassuring smile. When George was young, I'd always hoped he would do the same, but although as he got older I'd learned that he wouldn't, my heart still gave a twinge each year. Now I felt annoyed with myself: why couldn't I just accept that it wasn't George's way? I couldn't make him something he wasn't and George always knew I was in the audience, which was all that mattered. When he stepped on the stage in just a minute, he'd know I was watching. Then we'd go home, have a biscuit with Ben and go out to turn on the wonderland lights.

George had been practicing for weeks. At first he'd told me that he didn't want to be in the concert because he didn't want people staring at him. Then he'd told me he was sick of giving up his lunch break for rehearsals—Marjorie Kinnan went to town at Christmas every year and all the children took part. Now the day itself had arrived and I had a stomach filled with butterflies and a head pounding with nerves. Would George sing? Or would he refuse and stand silent amid all his classmates? Some of them were playing instruments as the parents waited for the concert to start, and as kids started filing on stage, I sat up extra tall to see George. I didn't know when he'd be coming on, so my eyes were darting everywhere until I saw him.

George had his head down. He was holding a light in one hand and wore a red T-shirt. I so wanted him to sing and as he took his position on stage and the music started, I looked at him, willing him to join in as his classmates began singing. Then suddenly he opened his mouth, and as excitement rushed through me I made the ultimate mum mistake and my hand shot up in the air to wave at him. I just couldn't help myself as I thought back to all the school events he hadn't taken part in, the concerts or plays where he'd stayed stock still and silent. Now George was joining in at last.

The moment he saw my hand go up, his eyebrows shot up too and I stopped waving: I didn't want to put him off. It was hard to contain myself, though, as I watched him sing and when the music finished, I jumped up and started clapping so hard I thought my hands might fall off. George looked around at the hall full of people. I knew he wouldn't like all the noise of the applause but as I wiggled around in excitement, feeling as if I was going to burst at the sight of him, he looked at me. Then as his eyes locked with mine his mouth curled into a smile.

Best Christmas ever.

When the concert had finished and I'd stopped myself from making so much fuss that George would make sure he never took part in another one, we went home and opened the front door to find the house strangely quiet. Usually Ben ran to the door to meet us, but there was no sign of him tonight.

"Baboo?" George called and we started searching.

Ben wasn't in the living room or the kitchen, and the chair in my bedroom upstairs was empty; he wasn't lying on his pillow and there was no sign of him in George's room either. As I carried on hunting, George went downstairs to look again.

"He's decorating the tree," I heard him shout before he started laughing.

I ran downstairs and into the living room. I couldn't see Ben anywhere.

"He's there!" George said, pointing at the 6-foot tree that had pride of place in the corner of the lounge.

My eyes travelled up—and up—until I saw Ben's green eyes staring out from the very top of the tree. He was sitting surrounded by lights and baubles and gazing down. He was the Christmas cat surrounded by tinsel and decorations, and from high up in the Christmas tree, Ben looked down at us and miaowed. George and I started laughing.

"I think he likes the tree, Mum," George said.

"Maybe a bit too much," I replied. "Now shall we get him down?"

PART THREE

Losing Ben

Chapter 14

Maybe the months after the winter wonderland really were the best that George and Ben had together, or maybe that's just how I remember them. By the time we were getting ready to go on holiday in September 2009, I was worried that George was going to refuse to leave Ben, because they were even more inseparable than ever. But a friend I'd looked after during many years of ill health wanted to take us to Egypt and I knew it would be a dream come true for George to see the blue sea and fishes that he had loved for so long. Somehow I had to persuade him to go. I didn't have much luck at first: George refused to be budged. He just didn't want to leave Ben. It was only when Howard offered to move into our house while we were away to look after Ben that he finally agreed. Knowing Ben would be happy in his own home, George had told me he'd go away. Now our bags were waiting by the front door as we climbed the stairs to say goodbye.

Ben was asleep on his pink blanket as we walked into my bedroom. He was lying on the bed, looking so peaceful that I didn't want to wake him, and my heart turned over as I looked at him. Two weeks felt like such a long time now as George and I stood at the foot of the bed.

"I will never go away again," George said. "He knows I'm going. Ben's sad. That's why he's staying asleep because he knows we're leaving him, don't he?"

"He's going to be well looked after," I told George. "He's going to be here with your dad and he'll hardly know we've gone. We can ring him every day and Dad will put the phone on loudspeaker so that Ben can hear our voices. He's going to be fine."

As George sat down softly on the edge of the bed, Ben opened his eyes. Looking at us, he gave a long meow. It was the meow he used to say hello—a long one with two notes in it that he made whenever we came back from going out. Otherwise, Ben had a long but flat meow that he used when he was unhappy and a shorter one to say yes.

"I'm going to bring you lots of presents home," George said as he picked up Ben. "I'm going to bring you home some sand from the sea too."

His eyes filled with tears and I suddenly wondered if we should even be going away. Was I wrong to think that this trip was something we had to do together? Or should I have just stayed here where I knew George and Ben would be happy? I told myself to stop worrying. I knew we'd all miss each other, but how could we not go on a trip that George would remember forever? When he got to Egypt he would love it and have the time of his life.

I would be glad to get away as well because for some reason I didn't understand a man on the estate seemed to have really taken against me and George. I didn't know why but it felt like he was set on making us feel uncomfortable. Things had gotten so bad, in fact, that I'd almost started to dread leaving the house. Whenever I went out, it felt like his eyes were on me and it had all made me feel quite uneasy.

I'd tried to ignore it at first, hoping the man would give up if he didn't get any reaction. But then came the day when George's school bus pulled up outside our house one afternoon and something happened that made me realize I couldn't turn a blind eye anymore.

I was folding the washing upstairs when I heard the rumble of the bus and Ben curled around my feet as I walked to the window to wave hello. But as I went to call out to George, I saw the man stop as he walked down the road past our house. Then he started laughing as George walked past him to go up our drive.

"Oy, window licker," he suddenly cried. "Learned anything at school today? Did you have a good time on the funny bus with all the dribblers?"

I stayed completely still.

"It's the special bus," I heard George say to the man as he walked toward our front door. "The special bus for my special needs school."

"Oh yeah. Really special. Specially for window lickers."

Rage boiled up inside me as I watched the man laugh. How could he speak like that to George? How could he say those things to a child? George didn't say a word as I opened the front door and he walked into the house.

"Why don't you watch a bit of TV and I'll get you a drink?" I said and closed the lounge door behind him before marching out of the house to where the man was still standing. George was going to have to learn to fight his own battles one day but it wasn't going to be this afternoon. Enough was enough.

"I've heard what you just said and I'm disgusted," I called to the man as he started walking up the road.

He turned around and laughed. I felt the anger rising higher inside me. I knew his kind: the kind who had fights and feuds with people, picked on those weaker than themselves and gave council estates a bad name.

"You should be ashamed of yourself," I cried, my temper rising even more. "You're a disgrace. How dare you speak to my son like that?"

The man looked at me. He seemed a bit less brave now he could see how revved up I was.

"Leave my son alone," I told him. "It's disgusting that you'd talk to him like that and if I ever hear you do it again then you'll have me to deal with. I don't know what we've done to upset you but whatever it is I'm sick of it. Just leave us alone."

With that, I had turned on my heel and marched back inside. I'd probably just caused myself a whole new set of problems, but I wasn't going to keep silent. That man had to be told right from wrong.

George was waiting for me when I walked back inside. He'd been standing at the kitchen window and heard everything.

"Don't bother, Mum," he told me. "I don't care. It's sad to call the people on my bus window lickers."

I took a deep breath as I tried to calm myself down.

"Some of the kids on my bus are really sick," George said. "But I'm not."

He walked back to the lounge, talking to Ben as he went. "Coward's the name. Picking on someone who can't fight back. Coward, coward."

We didn't say any more about it and I hoped George would forget, because when he got anxious it could take days to calm him down and he hardly slept or ate. But even though George didn't mention the incident again, it had obviously upset him.

"Does he understand? Does he understand?" he said to Ben during the days that followed. "Does he know what it's like for these children? Does he know?"

It wasn't that the man had upset George himself. He just couldn't understand how he could be nasty about children like his classmates. When the man taunted him, George knew he was being cruel. So a few days later, I went to try to talk to him about what had happened.

"You're going to meet people like that man sometimes, George, and you just need to ignore them," I said softly.

George watched Ben as he strolled into the living room and looked at us.

"I'm not bothered," he said. "They're nice souls, aren't they?"

"Who?"

"The children on my bus. Can they help being born like that? No. They're good souls."

"Do you know what a soul is, George?"

"Yes. It's a being, it's who's inside."

Ben jumped on to the sofa next to him and curled up, starting to purr. Knowing I couldn't ask George how he felt, I decided to tell him how I did.

"What that man said about your friends made me want to cry. It wasn't nice at all."

George looked at me. "Don't worry, Mum. People think they're window lickers because Joshua dribbles on the window. But he's nice. I like him and Ben does too."

Ben flexed his claws in and out against George's leg as he spoke, as if to reassure him that everything was going to be all right.

"Well, I think that if you and Ben like your friends on the bus that's all that matters," I said.

"They're nice souls, they are."

"I know, George."

"Nice souls."

But although George seemed to forget what had happened after that day, the man didn't and things had gone from bad to worse, as he even tried dragging Ben into the argument.

"What would your boy do without that cat?" he'd crow as I walked past him. "He'd be lost without him, wouldn't he? He does everything with that cat."

Or sometimes I'd hear him laughing as he went by my house.

"Here, kitty kitty," he'd call out. "Are you going to come and see me?"

Ben never went near the man because he knew what he was like and I didn't confront him again. As long as he didn't speak to George, I hoped that ignoring him would make sure he got bored of whatever game he was playing.

But even so, I was breathing a sigh of relief that George and I were going to Egypt. I'd heard that the man was going to move off the estate while we were away, which would finally mean an end to all the bad feelings. As I looked at George cuddling Ben goodbye, I couldn't wait to get away.

"I love you, you love me," George said, holding on to him tightly. "Do you want a kiss? I'm going on holiday to see the fish like Nemo. You're staying here and you will be busy busy with Dad and playing Xbox."

I walked over to the bed and bent down to kiss Ben so hard that he batted at me with his paw. I would miss him so much.

"We need to go, George," I said. "We don't want to miss the plane."

"I miss you already," he said to Ben as we walked to the bedroom door.

We stopped to smile at him one last time.

"We'll be back soon, Baboo," I said to him.

Ben gave us a long final look with his peaceful eyes as he lay on the bed.

Have fun. I will be fine here. I'm going to miss you but I want you to have the best holiday ever.

"I miss you already," George said to Ben again as I pulled the door gently closed.

It was the evening of our second day in Egypt and George had loved every minute on the beach so far. We'd gotten back to our apartment a couple of hours ago and he'd just finished helping me feed one of the stray cats he'd already made friends with.

"Ben would like us to look after them," George had told me as I scooped ham on to a plate for the strays.

I understood how he felt because I was missing Ben almost as much as he was. The first thing I'd done when we arrived the night before was phone Mum to check that he was OK—she was helping Howard look after him.

"Did he have his dinner early evening and then his supper just before bed?" I asked her. "Does he look sad or is he his usual self?"

"Ben's fine, Ju," Mum told me. "Now just relax."

Earlier in the day, I'd even got a text from Wendy to reassure me that Ben was fine and I'd told myself to relax as I stretched out on a sun lounger. It was just so strange to be without him. I almost expected to see him appear on top of a sand dune or something.

Now my mobile phone started ringing and I picked it up absentmindedly as I thought of Ben in a Lawrence of Arabia outfit on top of a camel.

"Ju?" a voice said. "It's Howard."

"Hello!" I said as George wandered out of the kitchen. "How's Baboo?"

"Well, that's why I wanted to ring," Howard said.

My stomach turned with unease. "What's happened?"

"I'm not sure, Ju. But I haven't seen him since yesterday evening and I thought you'd want to know."

"What do you mean?"

"I put him out last thing as usual in the front garden but he'd gone by the time I went back a couple of minutes later."

"What do you mean?" I asked. "Gone where?"

I couldn't understand what Howard was saying. Ben never went anywhere. Each night, he'd walk down our drive, across to Wendy's, back under my car and then on to the front doorstep. He did the same thing every evening.

"I don't know," Howard said. "I looked for him for hours last night and then again today. Your family have been round looking, and so have Wendy and Keith. We just can't find him. One minute he was there and then he was gone. It's like he's disappeared."

Something was terribly wrong. Ben never went off. He was too old to look for adventures and he wasn't one of those cats who went hunting for days or had a few meals at someone else's house because he fancied a change. He loved his home and didn't usually do more than nip out into the garden or on to the driveway. My body felt cold and shaky.

"I don't understand," I whispered to Howard. "Ben can't have gone."

"I know, Ju. But he has."

I hardly heard the rest of what Howard had to say and felt numb as I put down the phone, dazed almost, after he told me he'd phone later with any news.

Ben couldn't be gone. He couldn't have run away. We couldn't be without him. It just wasn't possible. He had to come home.

Sobs started to rip out of me and my breath came short and jagged. I felt sick. I couldn't think straight. This couldn't be happening.

"Can I have some juice, Mum?" George asked as he walked into the kitchen.

I could not speak as he stared at my white face. I had to get home. I had to start looking for Ben. He must be somewhere. He couldn't have just disappeared into thin air. I could not tell George that Ben had gone.

"Mum?" he asked again.

I looked at his face, so happy and peaceful. How was I going to tell him this news? What words could I find to explain that Ben had disappeared and reassure him that he would be found? Even as I looked at George and wondered what to say, I knew that no words can stop a world falling apart when you know for sure that it's about to.

"Baboo! Baboo!"

It was getting light as George and I scrabbled down the riverbank. We'd gotten back from holiday a couple of hours earlier after getting an emergency flight home. I knew some people wouldn't have left a holiday to look for their cat, but we didn't have a choice. The stabbing pain in my heart told me everything I needed to know. Ben was so much more to George and me than just a cat. He was as loved as any person, and I couldn't stay another minute in Egypt knowing he was missing.

The news had tumbled out when George had found me with the phone in my hand after I'd spoken to Howard. I was crying and trembling as I told him; huge sobs rushed out of me in jagged gasps. George just looked at me. He'd never seen me cry properly before.

"Ben is missing," I blurted out, unable to think clearly.

George was silent for a few seconds before speaking.

"He is probably dead," he said and walked away.

His words cut deep into me and I stood completely still as George went into the bathroom and shut the door. It just wasn't possible. It couldn't be. Ben could not be dead. I knew I had to calm myself down. I took deep breaths and tried to stop crying before going to talk to George again. After persuading him to come out of the bathroom, I sat him down and he looked at my face, blotchy and red with tears. I knew it would scare him and I breathed even harder to try to speak normally.

"I'm going to go home so that I can look for Ben," I said at last. "I know I will be able to find him."

George got up and a minute later I heard a rumbling sound as he reappeared, pulling his suitcase behind him. He had a couple of T-shirts in his hand and I knew I had to get us on a flight as soon as possible.

It had taken two days to organize it all and George had hardly spoken a word as we waited. Time had dragged by silently, both of us lost in our thoughts. The only thing that told me of the pain and panic George was feeling was the sight of his hands flexed out rigid beside him. It was something he'd done when he was younger if he got anxious. I kept trying to tell him that we would find Ben as soon as we got home, but he would not listen.

Neither of us had spoken on the flight home or during the drive back to the house. The moment I'd opened the front door, George had run upstairs to search all of Ben's usual hiding places while I walked out into the garden to call him. I couldn't think of what else to do, but I had to do something because the more I'd thought about it, the more convinced I was that someone had taken Ben to play a joke on us. He'd been outside our house one minute and gone the next. Someone must have done something.

"No one would do that, Ju," Mum had told me when I'd phoned to tell her. "It would be too cruel."

"But why else has he disappeared, Mum?" I'd wailed.

"He might just have gone off in a huff when you and George disappeared. You know how cats can be."

"But Ben's not like other cats!'

"I know, Ju. He'll be back. I know he will."

As we had traveled home, I'd clung to the hope that Ben would come running at the sound of our familiar voices. But calling his name in the garden did not bring him back and George couldn't find him anywhere in the house. Even though it was three o'clock in the morning, I could not bear to wait until it was light to start searching and put on my coat, telling George I was going out.

"He'll be at the river," he said, coming downstairs. "He likes it there."

It was as good a place to start as any, so I'd grabbed a box of Ben's biscuits and left the house with George. Everything was quiet and still as we walked to the river. There wasn't a person or a car in sight. It felt as though George and I were the only two people in the world, searching for the one we loved most.

"I think Ben's hiding," I said to George. "He's just playing a joke on us and all we have to do is find him."

But George said just two words again and again as we walked.

"He's dead. He's dead. He's dead. He's dead."

His words cut through me. George seemed so certain, but I couldn't bring myself to even consider the possibility that Ben could be dead. I wanted to tell George to stop saying it, to insist that it couldn't be, as we walked up and down the riverbank for what felt like hours, calling Ben's name and searching in the undergrowth. But there was no sign of him. After a couple of hours I told George that it was time to go home. He did not say a word as we trudged back but when we got home he went straight into the garden and stared at the summerhouse, as if willing his friend to be sitting inside as he usually was. Everything looked the same—Ben's chair was covered in his fur and his mouse wand was in his toy box in the living room—but it was completely different too. The house felt so still and empty without Ben's purr or the soft padding of his feet as he ran up to have a cuddle.

I walked outside to where George was standing. The sun was coming up and the clouds were ringed pink in the sky. Today was a new day and I'd start searching properly for Ben. He had to be somewhere close by. Whatever had happened to him, he could not be far. Ben couldn't have just disappeared into thin air. Someone must have seen him. I had to be like a detective and follow all the clues to find the person who had seen him last because that would lead us to him.

As I walked out into the garden, George turned to look at me. His eyes were completely cold.

"You've done this," he said. "It was you. You wanted to go away and now Ben's gone. It's your fault."

I froze inside. I knew exactly why George was blaming me. I was the one who'd persuaded him to go on holiday. I was the one who'd told him that Ben would be fine without us. Guilt flooded through me as I wondered if George was right. Why had I ever persuaded him to go away? Why couldn't I just have been happy with the way things were?

George pushed hard against me as he turned to walk back inside and I wanted to grab on to him as he disappeared, tell him that I'd find Ben as soon as I could. But I couldn't touch George, however desperate I felt. Something had shifted between us now that Ben had gone.

Everything seemed so still, as if all the life had drained from our home. It felt unreal, unbelievable. I couldn't understand why Ben wasn't running up to me and meowing, or stretching out on a patio chair to catch the first sun of the day. I walked slowly inside and went up to George's room. The door was closed and behind it there was only silence. I took a deep breath.

"I'm going to find Ben," I said. "I promise you I will."

The door stayed shut.

"No, you won't," I heard George say eventually.

"I will. I promise you. I'll find Ben and bring him home."

I walked back along the landing and stopped outside my bedroom door. Ben's blanket was still lying on my bed, just as it had been when we left, and I remembered the last time I'd seen him lying on it a few days ago. Then I thought of George and the promise I had made him, a promise I wasn't sure that I could keep. All I knew was that I had to. You see, Ben wasn't just a cat: he was George's window on to the world, the key to the door which unlocked him. Call me daft, but he was like my second son, so I had to find him now that he'd gone missing. Because if not, I was more scared than I can say that I would never see the light in George's eyes again. There was only one way to make sure that it came back: I had to bring Ben home.

Chapter 15

George had stayed in his bedroom the whole of the next day and refused to come out as the house filled up with people who were going to help me start the search for Ben. Wendy and Keith had come over, Mum was there with Sandra and Boy, who'd taken the day off driving his cab, and Nob was coming over as soon as he finished work. As I rushed around, all of them were telling me not to panic.

"He won't be far," Boy kept saying as the printer gushed out page after page of a poster I'd made with a picture of Ben and my phone number on it.

"He'll be back before we get all these up," Mum said.

I knew they thought I was overreacting, that cats went off and Ben would come home, but I was certain he'd never do that. Ben had not been seen for four days now and I knew he needed help. Otherwise he would have come home. He wouldn't leave us—he loved George too much.

199

Earlier I'd gone to see George and found him sitting on his bed with his box of favorite shiny things in front of him—crystals, earrings and bottle tops that he'd collected over the years. He had refused to speak. I knew he'd be up there now lining all his precious shinies along a shelf one by one, trying to create order when all he felt was chaos. He was shut down, lost inside himself, and if I did not find Ben I didn't know how I was going to reach him again.

It takes only a moment to lose something precious and another to realize it's gone. The second I'd looked into George's eyes last night, I'd known what had been taken from me and just how far George had come with Ben. I'd gotten so used to our cat talk and laughs, George's special way of hugging me and the way he talked about love, and the nights when we'd watched TV together or sung old songs, that I'd slowly forgotten to appreciate all those things. But now they had gone and George blamed me for losing Ben. I felt afraid, panicked. Without Ben, I was sure that George would go back to how he had been before Ben came into our lives—a child who was almost a stranger to me—and I knew that I would not be able to bear it.

I'd started the official search for Ben that morning by registering him on missing pet Web sites. Wendy and Keith had helped me do this and they were going to set up Ben's very own Facebook page too—anything to help jog someone's memory of seeing a black cat with a white bib. I'd also gotten lots of useful advice from the Internet on how to find a missing pet. Ben's blankets were now outside, blowing on the washing line, lifting his scent on to the breeze to try to call him home. I'd even vacuumed the whole house and gone down to the river to scatter the contents, in the hope that he might smell home; and there was fresh mackerel hanging on pieces of string in the garden because I'd read it might help.

I tried to force myself to concentrate as I laminated posters and leaflets explaining there was a £250 reward for the person who found Ben. As thoughts of him kept running through my head, I hoped the reward would encourage all the kids in the area to look for him. Last night I had been so sure that he had been deliberately taken but now I could not stop thinking of all the other possibilities. Was he lying in a ditch somewhere, hurt? Had someone hit him with their car? I almost couldn't breathe when I thought of him hurt and alone, lying somewhere, waiting for us to rescue him.

When the posters were done and everyone had been given a bag of them, we set off in separate directions to put them up, leaving George at home with Mum. We had to make sure that everyone knew about our search; then it would surely be just a matter of time before someone phoned with the clue that would lead us to Ben.

A few hours later I arrived home, after going to cafés and shops, pubs and post offices, schools and libraries, to see a familiar figure walking down our road as I got out of the car. It was the man I'd had all the problems with, and although we hadn't spoken since the day I'd confronted him about what he'd said to George, I'd talk to anyone now if there was any chance they might help us find Ben.

"My cat's gone missing," I said in a rush as the man walked past our drive.

He stopped but didn't say a word.

"I've been putting up posters everywhere but if you see him then can you let me know?" I asked.

The man's mouth curled into a grin as I started to cry, tears bubbling out of me as I looked at him.

"Ben's not just a cat," I said. "He's far, far more than that. My boy can't live without him. We've got to find him. George is lost without him. Ben's everything to us."

The man stared at me even harder.

"Good luck with finding your pussy cat," he said and smiled at me.

I swear it felt as if he was enjoying seeing me suffer. I felt sick as I stood on the pavement and watched him walk away. Did he know something about where Ben was? I'd never know. But someone did and if I just kept looking long enough then I was sure to find them.

My friends and family wanted to help me search for Ben, but they had jobs to go to and lives to lead. They did whatever they could, though. Kayleigh came over every day after school to help me put leaflets through doors, while Wendy kept an eye on George and Keith did the printing. Mum delivered leaflets and Nob, Tor and Boy all put up posters. Even Lewis helped and my friend from the estate, Tracey, her mum Anne and her daughter Eliza gave up hours of their time to go to a supermarket car park and put leaflets on every car windscreen. But when people were busy at work and school, I often went out to search for Ben alone. Each day began to follow the same pattern: I'd get up, try to persuade George to eat some breakfast but he'd always refuse, and Mum would come over to watch him because he was still too upset to go back to school. Then I'd go out to put up posters and I spent hours every day driving everywhere I could think of to give out leaflets.

A week after we got home I was out on the estate when I saw one of our local community police officers. I knew him quite well because he'd come round to my house for cups of tea or to use the loo when he was walking the beat. Relief flooded into me the moment I saw him. The officer had always seemed really interested in our estate and all the goings on, so maybe he'd be able to help me.

"I thought you were on holiday, Julia," he said as I walked up to where he was standing with a woman officer I did not know.

"I was. But Ben has gone missing and I can't get rid of the feeling that someone took him. He just disappeared into thin air. It doesn't make sense. He's never gone further than the bottom of the drive before. I was hoping you might be able to have a quiet chat around the estate for me just to see if you can find anything out."

The policeman said nothing as he shifted on his heels uncomfortably.

"I think you need to find help somewhere else with that," he told me eventually.

I stared at him in shock. I knew this officer well. He had sat in my house at Halloween, quite happy to chat to me about everything under the sun, and now he wasn't willing to at least try to help me sort this out. I didn't want him to arrest anyone or anything. But as my mouth opened and closed like a goldfish and I wondered what to say, I noticed that the woman with him was smirking and saw red.

"What are you laughing at?" I growled.

"I'm sorry," the woman officer replied. "It's just that you're looking for a cat and they can disappear for weeks on end before coming home again, can't they?"

I was getting sick of hearing people say that, and although most meant it well, I knew this woman didn't.

"Not my cat," I told her angrily. "He wouldn't just disappear."

The woman officer carried on smiling at me, as though I was a bit simple, and then she looked down at the leaflet I'd given her.

"Sorry, but I can't carry this when I'm on duty," she said as she handed it back to me.

That was it.

"You can't even be bothered to carry a leaflet, you fat bitch?" I said under my breath.

It was terrible, I know, but all I can say is that everyone is human and on that day I lost control of myself. The male officer looked at me in shock as I turned around without another word and walked home furiously. I could not believe how quick those officers had been to say no to helping me. Of course I didn't think that Ben's disappearance was top of the crime solving to-do list, but I didn't understand why they could not at least try to help. Politicians talk all the time these days about bobbies on the beat and community policing, but I was part of the community and these officers did not seem to care. The police were only too pleased to pile on to the estate in their vans if the local kids stepped out of line. But at least now I knew how things stood: I and the people who loved George were going to have to bring Ben home ourselves.

Excitement rushed through me as I ran to pick up the phone. Now people were seeing the posters the calls had started and each time one came I felt filled with hope that it would be the person who'd found Ben.

"Hello," a voice shouted as I picked up the receiver.

It sounded like an elderly man and I could hear a woman's voice in the background.

"Stop talking, Doris!" the old man boomed. "I'm trying to tell her, aren't I? Just let me get me words out."

"Hello?" I asked. "Can I help?"

"No, love. But I can help you. We've got your cat here. It's in our kitchen. We've seen your poster and we know it's him. He's looking at me right now."

"Is he black?" I asked, because I'd gotten a couple of calls from people who obviously had a bit of trouble reading and had rung to say they'd seen a gray or a tabby cat.

"Black as tar, love," the man told me. "Are you going to come and get him?"

I scribbled down the address he gave me before knocking on Wendy's door to ask if she would pop over and stay with George.

Five minutes later, I drew up outside a mid-terrace house with trees in the garden and a tiled step leading to the front door. Nerves filled me as I rang the bell. Was Ben inside? Would I be taking him home to George soon? I'd hoped that we'd find him quickly and now I knew I'd been right to think like that. Somehow Ben must have ended up here, just a couple of miles from home, and I was going to take him back to where he was meant to be, safe and sound after his adventure. The picture of him on the poster was so clear that it must be him.

The door was opened by an elderly man with a big belly, and a woman with white hair stood beside him in a hallway that was covered in such brightly colored wallpaper it made my eyes cross.

"Are you here for the cat?" the man said. "Come in, love. Come in. We knew it was him as soon as we saw him in the garden. He's not from around here, because we know all the cats and we've never seen him. He's friendly too. Not a stray. I knew he was lost. He was too fond of people to be a wild cat."

The man led me down the corridor and I suddenly felt nervous. Was Ben OK? He'd been gone for more than a week now, so if he hadn't had anything to eat he'd be starving. Night after night, I'd kept thinking back to when he first came to our garden, so weak and sick, scared and angry. I'd hardly been able to sleep for thinking about him and what a state he'd been in back then.

"He's through here," the man said. "It's him, I know it is."

He opened a door leading into the kitchen. It was neat as a pin and there was a teapot on the table, waiting to be filled.

"There he is," the old lady said with a smile.

I stared into the corner to see a pair of big green eyes looking up at me and my heart lifted. But a split second later I could see it wasn't Ben, however much I wanted it to be.

"Is he yours?" the man asked.

"No, I'm afraid not," I said, hoping that I wouldn't start crying.

"Really? I was sure it was. We've never seen him before, have we, Doris?"

The cat stared at us as we stood looking at him.

"What are we going to do?" the woman said. "We were so sure he was yours."

As I looked at the couple, I knew I couldn't just turn around and leave them to deal with the cat. I had to help, because maybe there was a family somewhere as frantic as I was, searching for their pet. My best hope was that it had been microchipped, just as Ben had been. A chip is the size of a grain of rice and is embedded in a cat's coat; it lists its name and owner's contact details. Every vet, police station and animal sanctuary has a chip reader, so if a cat gets lost anyone who finds it is able to trace its home. But lots of people don't realize that cats have them, which means they don't look for them, so I knew it didn't mean someone hadn't found Ben just because I hadn't had a call. Maybe I could help this cat find its home again and someone would do the same for Ben any day soon.

I scooped up the cat and put it in my car to take it to the vet. But it was only when I was halfway there that I wondered what I'd do if it wasn't chipped. I couldn't take the cat home with me. George would think I was playing a horrible joke or trying to persuade him to accept a replacement for Ben. A lovely woman had even phoned to offer us a kitten after reading Ben's missing poster, but I'd told her we couldn't have another cat. We just wanted Ben.

I need not have worried. When the vet ran his scanner over the cat, a number appeared on the screen that told us it had been chipped. The vet rang the microchip center, gave them the number and got the cat's details.

"Here's the address," he said and reeled it off.

Hold on a minute. I recognized that road. It was the one where the old couple lived. In fact, the cat lived next door to them. They'd only gone and captured their ruddy neighbor's cat, hadn't they?

"So whose is it, love?" the old man asked when I got back to the house. "Where's it from?"

I wasn't quite sure how to break the news.

"It comes from around here," I said, not wanting to be too specific with the details, to save them any embarrassment. "I think we should just let it back out into the garden and it will find its way home."

"But where's it from exactly? Did that chip thing tell you?"

It was time for the truth. "It's from next door."

The old man looked confused for a minute before bursting out laughing. "Well, I never. Did you hear that Doris? It's the neighbor's cat."

The elderly couple started laughing themselves silly as I stood on the doorstep.

"I'm so sorry," the woman said. "We've really wasted your time, haven't we?"

But they hadn't. As long as there were people like them, prepared to take time out of their day to read a poster and pick up the phone to try to help, I was sure that Ben would be coming home any day soon.

The kindness of strangers can be an amazing thing. In the first few weeks after starting my search, I met some wonderful people—cat lovers just like me who all wanted to help find Ben. There was Freda, an older lady who phoned regularly to see if there was any news and tell me she was saying prayers for us; Marina, who lived in the area and had also lost a cat, so we kept each other updated on our searches; and Pat, who lived in Isleworth and had put up a huge noticeboard in her garden to advertise missing cats and help families who were lost themselves without their pet.

Then there were the people who had seen the poster and wanted to give me any kind of clue that might help find Ben because they knew how anxious we must be to find him. If only they knew the truth. I wasn't just anxious: I was getting more and more desperate, because George didn't want to go out or do anything. He didn't play or go into the garden. He just sat in his bedroom for hour after hour and had stopped eating a couple of days after we got home. Now he was hardly drinking either, and I kept an anxious eye on the plates of food which I found outside his bedroom door untouched, the glasses of water that he hardly sipped. He didn't want to do anything but be alone. I'd only managed to persuade him to go back to school after telling him that Ben would want him to go. Even then, I'd had to ask the driver, Maureen, to turn off the music that usually played on the bus because George couldn't bear anything that was happy. He just wanted everything to be as still and quiet as he was. Night after night, we sat in the silent house—me in the lounge and George upstairs in his bedroom—because all the life and laughter had disappeared from our home the moment Ben had gone.

"I hate you," George said again and again as he came home from school, went up to his room and left me feeling completely empty as he slammed the door shut.

To hear him say that after all the love we'd known during the past two years was unbearable and nothing I said made a difference. My tears came when I was alone with my thoughts and I knew that losing Ben meant I had lost George too. No matter how positive I was about my search, whatever I tried to tell George about it, he wouldn't listen. When he did finally leave his bedroom, he'd come downstairs to hover about in the background as I made up posters before looking at them and telling me the picture wasn't right.

"People won't recognize Ben," he'd say, so I asked him to pick out his favorite photo to use on the posters. It was a photo of Ben lying on a tartan rug. But the moment that George was happy with the posters, he went back to sitting alone for hour after hour. To him, it was simple: Ben had gone, which meant he was lost forever. Within a few days of getting home, George had started to cry, huge big sobs the like of which I'd never seen before. All the years that I'd spent wishing George could show me more of his emotions came back to haunt me as I watched grief pour out of him. I felt completely helpless. I had never seen him like this before. George had never really cried as a child and the only time he had shed tears was when I'd told him that an animal such as Mum's dog Polly or a person he knew had died. George understood it meant he would never see them again, but he always stopped crying almost as soon as he started. Now, though, he could not stop the tears, which wracked his whole body and made him tremble. I longed to comfort him but couldn't reach him as he mourned losing Ben, and I was shown in the most painful way I could ever have imagined just how deep his love was. George was suffering a pain the likes of which he had never known and there was nothing I could do to stop it.

"I can't breathe," he would say over and over as I tried to put food in front of him. "I can't swallow. My heart is coming out."

Some mornings, he'd walk into my bedroom and sob as he stood and looked at Ben's pillow on my bed. But he wouldn't ever let me anywhere near him or say a word except in anger when the rage he felt about what had happened flooded out of him.

"This is all your fault," he'd scream. "Ben's gone. Nobody likes me. I can't get on in the world. You done this."

As much as I knew Ben's disappearance was no one's fault, part of me also agreed with George that it was mine. I was the one who'd agreed to go away and all the guilt I'd struggled with throughout George's lifetime as I wondered if I was somehow responsible for his problems returned tenfold. When Ben had arrived, I'd felt as if I'd finally done something really right for George, but now as he looked at me with tears on his face and hate in his eyes, all the guilt I'd once felt came flooding back. I just wanted to cuddle him, to do anything to try to ease his pain. I longed so much to comfort George. But I couldn't, and I felt just as I had during all the years when he was young and nothing had reached him: so helpless and so desperate that I could hardly put my feelings into words.

"I'll find him, I promise you," I told George again and again. "I'll do whatever I have to. I'll win the lottery and put up a big reward."

"No you won't! He's gone and I hate you."

The only time George spoke to me now was when he got home from school and asked the same question as soon as he got through the door each day.

"Have you found him?"

And every day I had to tell him the same thing. "Not yet. But I will."

As I sat alone in the evening, I thought about Ben again and again. I longed to hear him meow, see the curve of his tail disappearing through the door and feel the weight of his soft paws landing on my lap as he jumped up for a cuddle. The ache I felt for him was matched by the fiery panic that was building inside me about the state of George. The only way I could keep it in check was by answering every phone call I got, in the hope that it might lead us to Ben. The calls were coming thick and fast now, as many as 30 some days, and I responded to each one by either phoning the person and getting enough information to know for sure that the cat wasn't Ben, or by taking down all the details and driving to the place if I couldn't be sure. I was out every day from the moment George left for school until he came home again, because most of the time I didn't manage to find the cat I had been called about so I had to keep going back until I did. Often I'd take food and ask the person to feed the cat at a certain time, hoping that I'd be able to see it then, or ask them to try to tempt it into a garage or shed so that I could have a look. But that wasn't possible a lot of the time, so I'd drop everything each time I got a call. Mum was getting used to being left in the middle of the supermarket when my phone rang. "Got to go," I would tell her as I sprinted off and left her standing in the cereal aisle.

There were so many calls because there were so many posters all over the area now that I'd started to widen the search to Feltham and Hayes to the west, and Richmond and Chiswick to the east. I'd put up so many that a man from the council had even told me I could get prosecuted for littering if I didn't stop, but at least I knew I was getting the message out.

One of the phone calls I got was from an Australian man who told me that he got on the train into central London each morning from Osterley station, about 4 miles down the road. Since around the time that Ben had disappeared, he had been seeing a black and white cat on the railway embankment most mornings. I knew feral cats were often found living close to railways, so I wondered if Ben might have followed them. I took down all the details before packing up a pile of leaflets and going to the streets around the station to post them through every door.

Within a day, I'd gotten an e-mail from a man living in one of the houses near the railway line who had been feeding a stray black and white cat. But although I kept going back to try to find it, the cat was never there, so I asked the man if he would take a picture when he next saw it. Hope filled me when he sent one. The cat certainly looked like Ben, but I couldn't be completely sure if it was him or not because the picture had been taken side on, so the distinctive white bib on his chest was hidden. I'd seen enough, though, to know that I had to find the cat. After going back a few times without success, I decided it was time for desperate measures. I asked Mum to come over to stay the night because I was going to stake out the railway bank under the cover of darkness.

"Are you certain about this, Ju?" Mum asked as I packed up some sandwiches and a blanket. "Do you really want to sit out there alone all night?"

"I've got to, Mum. I've got to know if it's Ben."

As darkness fell, I put a bowl of food beside the car. It was Ben's favorite, so he'd come running if he smelled it. But although several cats turned up for a quick bit of dinner, he wasn't one of them. As the hours ticked by and I kept running the engine to get a bit of warmth into the car, I felt so sure that he was somewhere close. But as I thought about it, I suddenly realized what I was doing wrong. How was Ben ever going to find me sitting in a Toyota Aygo?

Getting out of the car, I stared at the railway bank. Is that where he was hiding? Was he sitting in a bush or hiding in a tree there? As I walked toward the fence that ringed off the railway bank, I knew I could be arrested for trespassing if I went on to it, but as I climbed over I told myself it was a necessary crime.

"Baboo?" I called into the darkness.

I clambered through brambles and felt them scratching at my face, wondering for a moment what on earth I was doing: everyone else was fast asleep in their comfy beds and I was out here at the dead of night, all alone on a deserted railway embankment, trying to find a cat that might not even be Ben. But if that is what it took to find him I'd do it—and more—because I could not give up until I knew. I had to follow up every phone call and sighting, to keep believing, because there was no other choice.

I went up and down the railway embankment for hours, calling Ben's name, but I couldn't find any sign of him and had to go home in the end. But hours after I called the man who'd been feeding the stray to ask him to let me know when he saw it again, the phone rang.

My heart was battering in my chest as I jumped into my car. The man had only just seen the cat. It was on the embankment right now. Every minute I was in the car felt like an hour as I sped over to Osterley. After parking, I rushed to the fence next to the embankment and sure enough I could see a black cat in the distance, sitting in the grass without a care in the world. I strained my eyes to get a better look. The cat was so far away I couldn't tell if it was Ben or not, but I didn't want to scare it by getting too close too quickly.

"Ben?" I called. "Baboo?"

The cat started meandering up the railway bank, closer and closer to where I was standing, and my heart soared when I saw a glimpse of white on its chest. But at that moment, the cat moved its head and I noticed a bright red flash on its neck. It was wearing a collar. It couldn't be Ben. He didn't wear a collar because he always pulled them off, and the vet had explained that because he hadn't gotten used to one when he was young, we'd never be able to persuade him to keep one on. I felt empty as I stared down the railway bank, wishing I could close my eyes, tap my heels together three times and open them to find Ben in front of me. Instead tears started falling down my face and I turned to go home.

Every time the phone rang when George was at home, he'd appear at the top of the stairs like a shadow, listening to what was being said, or stand in the hallway as I switched on the answer machine.

"That might be our cat, that might be our cat," he'd chant as we listened to the messages.

I usually tried to keep him away as I turned on the answer machine, because we had had a couple of nasty messages from people who swore curses down the line because I'd put a leaflet on their windscreen. We'd also got a couple of calls that were even more upsetting: one from someone who said they'd seen a black and white cat jump off a tower block and another from a person who said just "Meow" until the answering machine was full of their horrible taunts. Because of that, I did not want George to listen, but when I tried to distract him, he got so angry that I often didn't have a choice but to let him.

That's why he was standing beside me as I saw the light flashing on the machine when we walked into the house one cold afternoon about three weeks after Ben had gone missing. Every day had dragged by since then and I'd counted each one, feeling panicked as one week turned into two and then three. Soon it would be a month since Ben had gone and it seemed like a lifetime.

I hit the switch to listen to the messages.

"Julia Romp?" a voice cried as the answer machine tape started playing.

It sounded high, almost manic. The person was cackling with laughter as they spoke.

"We've got Benny Boo here, Julia. He's with us here. He's in our flat. He's black with a white chest and he's here. We've got him and you won't get him back."

The person started giggling. They sounded almost mad, and as we listened to the horrible laughter, George fell to the floor.

"George?" I said as I bent down to him. "George?"

He lay completely still, staring into space, and I sat down beside him. Fear flooded over me as I looked at him. I'd always tried to protect George, to keep him away from people who wanted to hurt others and cause them pain. Now that world was pouring into our house and there was nothing I could do to stop it if I wanted to find Ben.

George's face was completely white as I spoke to him.

"Come on, darling. Shall we get you up? That person is just trying to have a nasty joke. They haven't really got Ben. Don't listen to them. They are not well. They don't know what they're saying."

I made sure not to touch George. I couldn't go near him now because from the moment we'd gotten home from holiday, he hadn't come to me for a hug or even rough played with me. He hadn't spoken in cat talk either, and when I'd done it a couple of times without thinking, he'd looked at me in disgust.

"We can't do that now," he said. "Ben's not here."

On another day, he had said something himself in cat talk by accident and his face had gone white the moment he spoke.

Now George started to cry as he curled into a ball, sobbing and sobbing as he lay on the floor.

"There are nasty people in the world," I said to him gently. "But they won't have Ben. He wouldn't have gone to anyone like that. You know how much he can see into people's hearts: he'd never trust anyone so cruel."

George did not listen, though, and when he finally stopped crying, he got up and walked toward the living room.

"I have to listen to the messages," I said as I followed him. "I can't ignore them because one day soon there'll be one from someone who knows where Ben is and we'll find him again."

George opened the door into the garden and walked outside, where he tiptoed across the stepping stones on the lawn before stopping on the last one, the one that led to the summerhouse, Ben's favorite place in the world. Then he opened his mouth and started to scream.

Chapter 16

My stomach turned over as the postman spoke. He'd been out on his rounds when he'd seen a cat lying in the road. It had been hit by a car.

"It's black and white," he said. "Like the one on the poster."

"Are you sure it's dead?" I asked, the words feeling stiff as I said them.

"Yes. It was very badly hurt. It's in the road now."

"Thank you for telling me."

"I'm so sorry."

I put down the phone and felt shaky as I picked it back up to ring Boy and ask him to come with me to find the cat. I couldn't do it alone because just as I hoped it might be Ben each time I got a phone call from someone who'd seen a cat in their garden or walking down a road, I now felt sick inside that this could be him. Deep down, I'd been waiting for a call like this. I knew cats often got hurt on the road and as the weeks had passed I had kept wondering if that was what had really happened to Ben. However much I wanted to believe he had been stolen, because that would mean he was still alive, I couldn't keep pretending there was no possibility that something even worse had happened. Now I felt scared. This cat that had been found on the road just couldn't be Ben, because George had finally begun to hope that he might really come home again.

It had started with a conversation we'd had in the middle of a troubled night. As on every other night now, George had been up for most of it, waking about every half an hour. After weeks without sleep we were both exhausted, and in the end I'd persuaded George to get into my bed to see if it might help. George hadn't wanted to at first, because it meant sleeping on Ben's side, but although I'd managed to convince him, he was soon out of bed again, pacing back and forth in front of the window and pulling the curtains back to look at the night sky.

"It's so dark," George said. "I wonder if Ben can find his way around. I can't find him. Is he cold? Is he in someone else's bed? Is he hungry?" The questions had gone on and on.

I'd tried to distract him. "Do you think Ben might have moved in with another family?" I'd asked.

It was something I hadn't really talked about to George, but I had kept thinking of all those stories I'd read in the newspapers about cats who went missing for months and then came home right as rain because a stranger had been feeding them. People had kept telling me that might have happened and now I was beginning to think they could be right. The more weeks that passed without any news, the more fear was building up inside me, and I was starting to believe that anything was possible—even that Ben might really have thought we'd left him when we went on holiday and run away himself.

"Could he have got into someone else's car or a removals lorry and been taken somewhere?" I said to George. "You hear about that on the news sometimes."

George stared outside. "No," he said. "He wouldn't go and live with anyone else."

But when I got up the next morning, I heard George talking as I got his breakfast.

"Ben might have moved somewhere else," he said quietly. "Baboo might have a new home."

It told me that hope was flickering inside him at last and I wanted to encourage it. We still didn't know anything for sure, and until we did I wanted George to hope—anything to stop the sadness that was draining him more and more each day.

"I'll find Ben if he is with another family," I told him. "He would have come home by now if he could, so I just need to bring him back to you."

But now doubts filled me as I phoned Boy and asked him to come and pick me up. Was I really right to have encouraged George to believe? It had been more than a month now with no sign of Ben. Maybe I was living in cloud cuckoo land? After Boy got to my house, we rushed to the address the postman had given us and I felt sick as we arrived there. But all we could find was a patch of bright red blood on the tarmac: the cat had already been taken off the road. I wanted to cry as I looked at it. We couldn't leave without knowing if it was Ben or not. So Boy and I started knocking on doors at opposite ends of the street to see if anyone knew where the cat had been taken. As I waited for one to open, I thought of George, his hope and this black and white cat that had lost its life. Panic washed over me as I thought what it would mean if it really was Ben.

"I hope you can help me," I said as a man opened the door. "A cat's been knocked down and I need to find it."

"It's here," the man replied, his face serious as he spoke.

A girl and a boy were standing beside him.

"I think it might be mine," I said.

"It's not. It's our cat. I've buried it in the garden."

"I'm sorry to ask, but are you sure? I was told the cat was badly hurt, so you might have made a mistake."

"No. I'm certain."

For just a few seconds, relief rushed through me. Then I felt guilty. How could I feel happy when this family had lost a pet they loved?

"I'm so sorry to bother you," I said, as the man closed the door and I turned to walk away.

I felt so shaken later that day as I told Mum about what had happened and the words rushed out of me as I told her that I couldn't help but think of Ben and what might have happened to him. Then I turned to see George standing by the door and realized he'd heard everything I'd said.

"The world's gone mad," he cried. "The cars are ruining the trees, there's no fresh air and the animals should be walking free. Why can the cars knock cats down?"

"Because sometimes accidents happen," I told him. "It's very sad but they do."

"We should get a cart and a horse to show other people that's better than a car."

"I'm not sure we could do that, George."

"But we're running out of oil. People can't breathe. The cars are killing us. The cars are killing cats."

The conversation went on and on over the next few days. I tried to calm George's worries and wished so much that he'd never heard me talking to Mum.

But although I kept telling him we didn't know what had happened to Ben and couldn't give up hope, I realized I might have gotten it all terribly wrong when George came to talk to me the day before Halloween.

"Don't worry, Mum," he said.

It was the first time he'd spoken to me like that since Ben had gone and I wondered what had happened to make him do so.

"Ben's coming home," George told me.

I wasn't sure what he meant.

"He's coming home tomorrow."

"Why tomorrow?"

"Because it's Halloween. He loves Halloween. He wouldn't not come home."

My heart sank. George was remembering our party last year and all the fun we'd had. He was convinced that Ben would come home to celebrate with us. For the whole of the next day, he was deep in thought, but as the morning of Halloween slipped into the afternoon and then evening came, I could see George falling back into the black pit of his sadness. Tor had kept telling me to reassure him, to stop him from disappearing into it. But I knew it was too late to keep George from going back there now. By the time evening came and trick or treaters started knocking on the door, George was tapping his fingers and anxiously chanting.

"Tell them to go away," he kept saying as the bell went again and again. "He's not here. He's not coming home."

In the end I turned off all the lights in the house to stop people knocking on the door. George and I spent the rest of the evening sitting in darkness. The silent house felt like a tomb surrounding us and guilt filled me. How was I ever going to make this right again if I didn't find Ben? How would I ever get back the boy I knew George could be? As I sat and thought, I realized two things: maybe I had been wrong to encourage George to hope, and from now on I had to be realistic about the possibility that Ben might not come back to us. But until I knew for sure that he wasn't, until I found the truth, I would keep believing that he might and telling George that I did. I had to have hope for the two of us now.

A good friend I made as I searched for Ben was a woman called Sally, who lived next door to her mum and aunt in Isleworth, just down the road from Hounslow. We met after Sally's mum phoned to tell me that she and her sister had been feeding a black and white cat since late September.

"We're sure it's yours," she said. "It's identical to the one on the poster."

So I rushed round as I always did, found the two ladies at home with their Scottie dog and saw immediately that the cat wasn't Ben: the only white fur it had was a splash at the end of its nose as if it had been dipped in white paint. But the cat was in such good condition that I was sure she belonged to someone. Feral cats and people's pets are very different: one's thin and scraggy, the other is well fed and fatter, one is able to let a person get near, the other runs a mile. So I suggested that I take this one to the vet to check for a chip.

"Don't worry," one of the ladies said to me. "Sally, my daughter, is away in America but she's coming home soon, so she can help us. She's been helping at an animal charity for years, so she'll know what to do."

I didn't expect to hear from them again, but Sally e-mailed when she got back from her holiday to apologize about the mix-up before explaining that the cat they'd been feeding had been nicknamed Dizzy. Sally was fostering her until the local animal charity found the cat a new home, and Dizzy's story soon had a happy ending. A family Sally had sat next to on the plane home from America, who lived just a couple of miles away, offered Dizzy a home.

She wasn't the only cat I met who had strangers to thank for giving it a new life, and three of the luckiest were Monty, Socks and Prudence. They belonged to a woman called Mavis, who I went to visit one evening in November with Wendy. Mavis had called to say she'd been feeding a stray matching Ben's description. The door of her house was opened by a woman in her seventies with silver hair cut into a neat bob. Mavis was very well presented and her house was the same—everything was just so, with the smell of clean laundry in the air and an ironing board folded in the corner of her kitchen.

Mavis told us that the first cat she'd taken in was a stray she'd called Monty when he came to live with her four years before. Then she'd adopted a cat she'd called Prudence, after finding her badly neglected and starving.

"I can't introduce you to Prudence today," Mavis told Wendy and me. "She's deaf and old and doesn't like strangers too much. She lives in one of the bedrooms upstairs and doesn't go out."

I could see that Mavis felt really protective of all her cats but especially Prudence. The latest addition to the family was a black and white cat called Socks that Mavis had been feeding since he had appeared in her garden a few weeks before. He was the one she wanted me to see, because although Mavis thought it probably wasn't Ben, she wanted me to see him for myself to make sure.

"It'll be time for his fish soon," she told us. "He has it every evening on the boardwalk." The boardwalk was a strip of wood just outside the back door.

Sure enough Socks soon appeared and, just as Mavis had thought, it wasn't Ben. I felt a wave of sadness. It had been nearly two months without him, but I still hoped that every cat I was called to might just be Ben. I could not stop myself from believing that I could find him if only I looked hard enough. But I pushed down my sadness as we stood chatting to Mavis. I could see that she was worried about Socks, who she was sure had a home somewhere.

"If my Monty wandered off I'd want someone to check if he was chipped, but I haven't been able to catch Socks," she told us.

I understood exactly how Mavis felt.

"Why don't I catch him and take him to the vet to get him checked?" I asked her and Mavis agreed.

Now the reason I could say that was because I'd become so determined to solve the mystery of the missing cat that I didn't just stop with Ben anymore. After coming across so many strays, I'd started catching some and taking them to the vet at the local animal charity to be checked for a chip, in the hope that I might track down their home for them. Sadly none of the half-dozen cats I'd taken in had had a chip, so I had taken each one back to where I found it, just as the charity had advised me to. That was why I could offer to help Mavis. I told her I'd be back the next day, armed with my carrier and some gloves, because I'd learned to be prepared for cat catching. I wasn't too worried about catching Socks; I knew what I was doing.

The next day I went back to see Mavis and asked her to put down a dish of food in the kitchen to tempt Socks inside while I hid behind the back door. She would close it when he came in and I would catch him.

Our plan went like clockwork. Socks appeared right on time and, after standing at the threshold and sniffing, stepped into the kitchen. Quick as a flash, Mavis slammed the door shut and I went to grab Socks. But the second he realized he was trapped, Socks went wild. I'd never seen anything like it. He flew into the air, jumped on to the sideboard, flew off it again on to the floor and reared up at me, his claws and teeth bared. It was like catching a tiger. Although I'd heard the expression "spitting like a cat" before, I'd never seen one actually do it, but Socks did. I ended up wrestling him to the ground, where I held him by the scruff of the neck before getting him into the carrier. It was all for his own good, of course, but Socks couldn't see that and when I put the carrier into the car, he almost smashed his way through on the way to the vet. He was the Incredible Hulk of cats.

After taking Socks to the vet at the local charity that Sally had introduced me to, the Animal Rescue Center in Twickenham, I was told that he hadn't been chipped. Socks also needed a health overhaul and an operation to neuter him, because the vet was sure he was feral. After that, Socks would need to recuperate somewhere, and I decided to offer to have him at my house because Mavis was elderly and already had two cats to look after. I was worried, though, about how George would react, because although I'd taken three strays home overnight before taking them back to the place where I'd found them, I hadn't had a cat in the house for any length of time.

"My Mum tries to look after everyone's cat," George said angrily to Nob after I brought Socks home and put him in a basket in the downstairs loo. "She don't care about Ben anymore."

"Of course I do," I told him. "But Socks has had a sad life just as Ben had before he came to us. He hasn't got a mum and dad to look after him."

"You don't care," George shouted. "You've forgotten him."

He pushed past me to go upstairs and I watched him disappear. George's anger was getting worse with each day that passed and it reminded me of the darkest days when he was young. Rage and frustration were pouring out of him now, just as they had back then, and I was the person who had done this because I was the one who had made us go away. Watching George wrestle with his pain was almost more than I could bear.

It was a hard week as Socks recuperated. George refused to even look at him. Socks was a cat—and Ben had never been just one of those.

"I don't need to look at it," George would tell me when I asked if he'd like to go and see Socks.

So I looked after Socks and the cat was as nervous as ever when I went to see him. I often came out of the loo with a couple of scratch marks and as soon as Socks was well enough, I took him back to Mavis's garden where he obviously felt most at home. During his stay with the vet, he'd been chipped and Mavis and I were now listed as his foster parents. I was happy for her when Socks finally disappeared down the garden because we both knew he'd be back for his fish that night. Mavis and I had been through a lot together for that cat, and as we walked back inside, she turned to me.

"Would you like to meet Prudence?" she said.

I knew by now that Mavis never let anyone see Prudence and I felt very honored as we tiptoed up the stairs to stand outside a closed bedroom door. Mavis opened it and I saw a beautiful room with a huge bay window, pink carpet and a bed covered in a pink eiderdown. The bedroom was so nice that I could have moved in there myself.

Prudence was lying on a pink cat bed in the corner, and as soon as the door opened, she got up to see who her visitors were. I forgot the rest of the room as I looked at her. Prudence was the most beautiful fluffy tortoiseshell with huge big eyes. She walked delicately across the room, putting each foot carefully in front of the other like a ballet dancer. She kept her nose in the air as she walked toward us before looking around as if to ask me whether I liked her bedroom. She was like royalty, not a Heinz 57 with a bit of moggy thrown in for good measure like most of the cats I knew. And as Mavis bent down to pet Prudence, I felt that it was only fitting for a cat who'd had such a bad start in life to end her days in a room fit for a cat queen.

I might have been Ace Ventura, Pet Detective, when I first started searching for Ben but I ended up more like Indiana Jones. All I could think was that the next call might be the one that helped me find Ben, the next cat I went out to find after someone caught a glimpse of it could be him; I had to chase any piece of information, however tiny, that might lead me to him.

As one month without Ben turned into two and December drew ever closer, my head was filled with fears about what might have happened, and the more my imagination ran wild, the more extreme my search got. My hope that Ben would come home was now balanced with my fears that something had happened to him, and whichever one it was, I had to know for sure. I could not break George's heart beyond repair by telling him Ben would not be coming home unless I was certain he would not be. George needed an answer, a full stop, and there was nothing I wouldn't do to get that for him. The worry of it all had made my hair start to fall out and the doctor had told me the bald patch on my forehead was caused by stress. I knew my hair wasn't going to grow back until I had found out what had happened to Ben.

Soon after he had gone missing, I'd started visiting the council yard where all the rubbish trucks and cleansing teams were based, because as well as sweeping the roads and picking up litter, they were responsible for disposing of any animals that were found after being hit by a car—which usually meant cats. After the bodies were picked up, they were put in a big plastic bag, taken to the yard, scanned for a chip and put into a freezer. If the cat was chipped, its owners were contacted to ask if they wanted their pet. If it was not, it stayed in the freezer until the council was sure it was unclaimed and then it was cremated. That happened often, because most cats weren't chipped. Even though Ben was, I couldn't get rid of the nagging idea that there might have been a problem with his, which would mean I'd never know if he was found on a road somewhere. I knew it was a far-fetched idea, but the head doesn't always rule the heart, so I went down to the yard every day just to make sure.

I wasn't allowed to see the cats myself. Instead a poor Australian man who worked in the office at the yard had to describe each one to me. I think he'd got a bit sick of my endless questions after about the first week.

"The tabby is chipped," he'd tell me. "Then there's a ginger but that's not yours. There was one found in Brentford but it's white."

In the end, the man kept being very busy whenever I turned up, but I'd just sit and wait until he saw me. I knew people found it a bit strange that I was so desperate to find a lost cat. In fact, the dustmen knew me so well by now that one of them meowed when he saw me. Nob had told me that some people were beginning to wonder about me, but I couldn't let it worry me. How could anyone possibly understand what Ben meant to me and George? People might think I was ridiculous, but I was just doing what had to be done.

Night after night George would go to my bedroom

window, where he had once stood to call Ben inside, and I would watch as he stood with his back to me and his body shook while he cried, his shoulders jerking. Each breath that ripped out of him sent a wave of panic through me.

"Do you think he's out there?" George would ask as he sobbed.

"Yes," I'd tell him. "And I'm going to find him."

"I kissed his nose," George said as if I hadn't spoken. "I rubbed his ears, I told him I was going on holiday to see the fishes and then he left me. He's gone."

Sometimes I tried to tell him about all I was doing to find Ben. But he didn't want to listen, so I would stand quietly with him—sometimes for up to an hour—until he finally stopped crying. Once I'd had Ben to help me comfort George or bring him out of himself, discipline him or make him laugh. Now there was no one but me and my voice was not enough.

"He will never be here again," George would say when he finally turned away from the window.

"Would you like a cuddle?" I'd ask him softly, hoping each time that he might let me near him.

"No. Don't touch me."

"I'll find him, George. I'll keep looking."

"He's dead. Now leave me alone."

That was why I had to keep going. I didn't have any other choice.

It was during my trips to the depot that I'd met Norma, the local council dog warden. Tall and slim, with brown curly hair and glasses, she'd been doing her job for years. She wasn't what you'd call the cuddly type. In fact, she'd got so used to plain speaking and telling people to put their dogs on a lead, make sure they picked up their mess and generally what was what that she didn't mince words with anyone.

"There's six dead in the freezer today," Norma would say when I went to see her. "And none of them is chipped."

As I started wailing at the thought of all those poor animals who would now go to a pauper's grave because no one had chipped them, Norma would look at me.

"Are you all right?" she'd ask with a surprised look on her face.

"No!" I'd cry. "Why can't people just chip their cats?"

"Story of my life, love. It's like this day in, day out."

But however much Norma didn't seem to understand how soft I was about it all, she had a good heart. I lost count of how many posters she put up for me in the council canteen and on bulletin boards; she had also e-mailed all the charities and animal organizations she worked with to tell them about Ben.

Norma was just one of the many kind people I met. There was also the builder who'd fed a stray his lunchtime sandwiches as he rang to tell me he'd been seeing it around the site he was working on; and the youth leader from the estate who'd fed a cat all the ham she'd got for the kids' lunches because she thought it might be Ben. Neither of those cats turned out to be him, but I appreciated the help—just as I did the kindness of strangers who'd talked to me as I stood outside a supermarket giving out leaflets one Saturday. I'd decided the pet aisle was the place to find people who noticed the comings and goings of stray cats.

I hadn't been there long when a member of staff came to move me on.

"I'm really sorry but you can't hand out leaflets here," she said.

"I won't force them on anyone."

"I know. But we just don't allow it."

Then she whispered that no one would get too worried if I stood outside the front door of the shop as long as I made sure not to block it. So I went outside with my huge bag of leaflets and tried to give them out. But people wouldn't look me in the eye or come anywhere near as they rushed in and out of the shop, and I felt ready to cry even when I did manage to get a leaflet into someone's hand because they usually dropped it; seeing Ben's face being trodden into the pavement just made me even more upset. I told myself that I couldn't start weeping and wailing because it would put even more people off. I had to get a bit more direct.

"I'm not trying to sell you anything," I started shouting. "I just need to find my cat. Please take a leaflet and see if you can help."

Everything changed the moment I said that. When people realized what I was doing, they were only too happy to take a leaflet. One bloke with a huge beer belly even came up to give me a quick hug.

"Don't worry, love," he said. "He'll come home soon."

I met so many people that day who told me about the cats they'd loved and it made me feel better because I didn't feel quite so alone. Even the security guard ended up smiling at me, and they're not usually a barrel of laughs, are they? Most people can understand what it is to love an animal and feel lost without them. Some even knew how it felt to wonder if the world has ended when the animal you love so very much is gone.

It was because of that love that I'd run through all the

gardens on a terraced street in Whitton chasing a cat that hopped over the next fence the moment I touched down on someone's lawn, and gone to every church in the area to put Ben's name in the prayer books. All I could see was a picture of Ben's and George's happy faces in my mind as I walked the streets of Brentford for hours one freezing night in thunder and lightning because a woman was sure she'd seen Ben. As I wandered around, soaked to the skin, I knew I wasn't going to find him, but I just couldn't bring myself to give up yet. So I carried on walking until I was too exhausted to put one foot in front of the other, and only then did I finally go home.

Some days it felt as if I was being given a hundred bits of advice on how to find Ben and all of them were flying round my head. When someone told me cats could drown in rain barrels, I couldn't walk past one without looking in it; when someone else said they could get stuck in houses by going in through the cat flap when people were away and getting trapped, I started keeping an eye on houses on the estate that looked empty; and I can't tell you how many Neighborhood Watch people came out to make sure I wasn't up to no good when I went to areas where no one knew me and tramped around with a tin of biscuits shouting Ben's name. I didn't understand that, to be honest, because what kind of burglar would keep going back to the same place and drawing attention to themselves by shouting a cat's name?

That wasn't the end of it. Ben's face was plastered all over the Internet and I even got his picture in the local newspaper after putting an advertisement in and getting a call from a journalist. When someone told me that cats could get stuck up trees for weeks, I started staring into every one I saw, just to check I didn't see a familiar face 30 feet up. I even asked my neighbors if they'd had visitors who might have taken Ben home in their car by accident.

Deep down, I still could not get rid of the feeling that Ben was alive somewhere—however impossible it seemed—and that's why I had to go to every sighting. Mum was with me on the day I saw a cat in the distance and started chasing it. When it disappeared up an alleyway, we got back into the car as we wondered what to do next. Just then, the cat dashed past again and as it squeezed itself through a tiny hole at the bottom of a gate, I flung myself on to the ground to see where it had gone.

"I've lost it, Mum," I shouted back to her. "I can't see it anywhere."

Then I got struck by something as I stared at the garden in front of me and couldn't help but tell Mum, "They've done a lovely bit of planting here."

As I said that, I saw a foot appear on the other side of the gate. I pulled my head back far enough to stare up into a huge pair of nostrils. The homeowner had come out to see who was badgering his poor cat and I got the giggles so badly I couldn't get the words out to explain to him what on earth I was doing.

Those were just some of the things I did on my search and there were more—far more. The worst one? Probably the trip I made to the river each day because, try as I might, I couldn't stop wondering if Ben had drowned there. I went every single day, and it wasn't enough to just walk along the bank: I had to get into the river, just to make things really difficult. I made a huge mistake the first time I did it by wearing my wellies. After walking down a shallow stretch of the river, I could see that the water was about to get deeper and decided to get out next to a pub garden that was packed with people smoking. But as I tried to get on to the bank, water rushed over the tops of my wellies and I got so weighed down that I couldn't lift my feet. After standing there swaying for what felt like ages, I finally managed to drag myself on to the muddy riverbank, where a crowd of people stared at me.

"Going for a swim, love?" one asked.

"Training to cross the Channel?" another cried.

"Is it fish for tea tonight, then?" another voice said.

After that, Nob got me a pair of waders to wear in the river and I'd stroll by the old people who lived in the bungalows down the road every day carrying them.

"All right, Julia?" they'd cry when they saw me.

"Fine!" I'd shout back as they gazed at me, wondering if I'd finally lost my marbles.

It was either that or I was spreading the contents of my Hoover bag beside the river. Ben had been gone for so long now that there couldn't have been much of his scent left in the house, but I was still convinced it might help. Once again, the pensioners would smile when I walked past carrying my vacuum bag. But a man who lived on the estate obviously got a bit more worried when he kept seeing me either in the river or spreading dust around whenever he went for a walk with his dog.

"Are you OK?" he'd ask.

"Just looking for my cat."

"Really? Out here?"

"Oh yes."

"When did it go missing?"

"Two months ago."

"Well, I'd get out of the river because I don't think you'll find your cat in there now."

I think I managed to convince him that I was just about OK, but I was learning that there's almost nothing you won't consider doing if you want something badly enough. If I stopped looking I would have to accept that I could do nothing to help George, and I could never do that. I just had to keep going, keep searching, until I found Ben.

It was late November and I had to talk to George about Christmas. People were starting to put up their lights, and the shops were full of decorations and presents to buy. The staff and pupils at Marjorie Kinnan were also going to start rehearsing for the Christmas concert soon. I couldn't put off speaking to George about it all any longer. We had not talked about the plans we'd had last year for another winter wonderland because neither of us could do it without Ben. But while we usually started getting the inside of the house ready for Christmas in the middle of November, and would normally have at least two trees covered with baubles and lights up in the living room by now, we hadn't done a thing yet.

So when George got back from school one afternoon in early December and shut himself in his bedroom, I climbed the stairs to knock on his door.

"George?" I said as I opened it.

He was sitting on his bed with his shinies collection, rearranging them just as he had done again and again since

Ben had left, and he didn't look up when I walked in.

"There's something I want to talk to you about," I said as I sat down beside George.

He pulled himself a bit further away from me.

"I wanted to talk to you about Christmas," I said gently.

"No," George said. "Not if he's not here."

"But I'm sure Ben would want you to have fun."

George started to cry, big, fat tears rolling silently down his face. This was how he cried now, without making a single sound, and I'd see him with wet cheeks as he brushed his teeth or as I dressed him. Once he'd even cried as he looked at his fish fingers and I knew he was thinking about how much Ben liked them.

"It's OK to cry," I said. "We're both sad, aren't we?"

"This happens to me," George replied. "Tears just come."

"I know they do. They come to me too."

Neither of us said any more as we sat together. I was running out of ways to reassure George, to tell him that I would find Ben. When I tried to talk to him now about what I'd been doing to look for Ben, George did not want to listen.

I sat beside him, longing to take his hand as tears rose up in me too. I ached for George, all we'd had and the light that had shone out of him when Ben was with us and we were the three musketeers together.

"Go away," George suddenly cried, angry that I was still sitting beside him. "Leave me alone. Shut my door. You lost Ben. Get out."

My heart twisted inside me as I got up to leave. Then as I reached the door I stopped. I had to try once more to get through to him.

"Are you sure about Christmas?" I asked. "I really hope Ben will be back in time for it. Are you sure you don't want to get everything ready for him?"

"No!" George screamed. "There's no Christmas without Ben. Get out."

There was nothing more to say. George was further away than he'd ever been before and I was worried that soon I would never be able to bring him back to me. As he became more like a shadow with every day that passed, it felt as if I was seeing my own child give up on life itself. George's heart was wasting away inside him and mine was breaking too.

Chapter 17

Whenever the phone rang late at night, I'd run down to answer it. Sometimes it would be kids laughing and at others there would be silence. But this time there was someone on the other end, and I could hear the roar of traffic in the background as he spoke.

"I have seen your cat," he said. "It's in the road."

My heart turned over, just as it had done when the postman rang. I'd been called to two other dead cats since then and both had upset me just as much as the first. One was in Twickenham and by the time I got to it, a woman living nearby had already come out to get the cat off the road because it was hers. I watched her sadly as she walked away. The next was in nearby Kingsley Road. Two people had rung me to say that a cat had been hit by a car there. It had already been collected by the council cleansing team by the time I arrived, so I'd rushed round to the depot and waited two hours for the truck which had picked up the body to get back.

"Can I see the cat?" I asked the driver when I finally saw him, my heart drumming in my chest.

"I'm sorry but we've already disposed of the body," he told me.

Panic filled me when he said that. "What do you mean? You can't have. I've got to know if it's my cat or not."

"It was too badly hurt," the driver said sadly. "Its head was off and its body was crushed. We had to put it in the bins."

"But you shouldn't have done that! You should have brought it here."

"It was too badly hurt to bring back." Then the man explained that he'd seen all the posters of Ben and he looked at me with sadness in his eyes. "I'm pretty sure it was your cat," he said.

"But how could you know if it was so badly hurt?"

"I could see enough, love. I'm sorry but I really think it was yours."

My breath rushed out of me. After nearly three months of searching, Ben had died on a road five minutes from our house? I couldn't understand what he would have been doing there. If he had been so close to home, surely he would have got back to us somehow? I wouldn't believe it was him. I wouldn't listen to what this driver was telling me.

"Ben's got a white patch shaped like a butterfly under his nose," I insisted. "It's really unusual, so you couldn't miss it. Other cats are blotchy but he's not. Did you see that on the cat?"

"I'm sure it was him," the driver replied sadly.

But I went home angrily telling myself that I didn't know for sure if the cat was Ben and I wouldn't believe it was

242

until I did. The driver was so certain, though, that he'd even rung me later that day to tell me again what he thought.

"I want to put your mind at rest about all this," he said. "I know you've been looking for your cat and I'm a hundred percent sure the one we picked up today was him."

"Thank you, but we can't be sure and until we are I will keep on looking," I said firmly.

But although I tried to forget what the driver had said, I just couldn't. Thoughts of the cat kept going round and round and they still were when I picked up the phone to be told that another cat had been found dead.

"It's on Powdermill Lane," the man told me.

"Where?"

"By the mini roundabout."

If Wendy came over I could be there in minutes.

"I'll leave now," I said.

Five minutes later I was in the car and rang the man back to tell him I was on my way.

"I'll be there soon," I said. "Can you just stay with the cat until I get there?"

"I'm so sorry but I can't," the man said. "I've got to get the last bus home. The lady from the pub is here and she says she'll wait."

"Well, thank you for ringing."

"That's OK. I know who you are because my temple is praying for you. We have a poster with a picture of your cat."

As I got out of the car and stepped into the freezing night, I could see a woman standing in the road. At her feet was the body of a cat, which she was protecting from other cars to make sure it wasn't run over again. She must be the landlady of the pub, I thought, just as the man had told me on the phone, and I silently thanked her as I got some towels out of the boot of my car before running across the road.

"I'm so sorry," she said as I looked down at the cat's body.

It was covered with blood and I kneeled down beside it before gently moving its head to check if it was still breathing. The cat was still warm but it wasn't alive. It had gone, its life taken on a darkened road by a car that had driven on and left it to die alone. As I lifted it up, I could see it wasn't Ben, but I didn't feel relieved; I just felt empty. This cat was obviously loved, because it looked well looked after, and I started to cry as I wrapped it in the towels and thought of the family who it belonged to. Was this what had happened to Ben? Had he died with only strangers to look after him?

I stood up, holding the cat gently in my arms. I would take it to the vet tomorrow morning to see if it was chipped.

"At least you found him," the kind landlady said quietly as she patted me on the back. "I know it's hard, but you can take him home and give him a proper burial."

As I silently cried I didn't have the strength to tell her the cat wasn't mine. I was exhausted by all the months of searching, all the hopes that had been dashed again and again. How could I keep doing this? Keep hoping enough for both George and me, when all he wanted to do was give up? Why couldn't I just accept that Ben had gone?

"Thank you for all your help," I said as I started to walk away.

My tears turned freezing cold in the wind as I went back to the car. Maybe I should just finally accept that I was never going to find Ben. It had been nearly three months now and I knew people were beginning to think that I was wrong to keep hoping. After the cat had been picked up by the dustcart, I'd even wondered myself if I was, and I talked to Mum and Wendy about it.

"Do you think I'm wrong to keep believing and telling George that Ben will come home?" I'd asked them. "Should I just accept that I'll never find him and lie to George, just to give him a final answer?"

Mum and Wendy couldn't tell me what to do, of course, but I knew what they thought.

"You might have to think about it, Ju," Mum had told me. "You can't go on like this. Your life has got to get back to normal. You're making yourself ill with all this. You're not sleeping properly and you can't even get round the supermarket without rushing off. This has got to stop sometime and maybe it would be easier for George if it ended sooner rather than later."

I'd lain awake that night for hours as I thought about what Mum had said. Maybe she was right; maybe I should tell George a lie just to release him from the not knowing. I could burn newspapers and put the ashes in a pot before telling George that Ben had died and been cremated. Then we could dig a hole in the garden and get a stone to remember Ben by. At least then George would have somewhere to go to be with him and he would know for sure that he was gone. But when I'd woken up the next morning and seen the sunshine outside I hadn't been able to bring myself to tell the lie. I couldn't say those words to George and see the pain on his face when he heard them unless I knew for sure that I had to.

Now I opened the door of the car and laid the cat gently

on the passenger seat. It was too late to do anything more now, so I drove home, where I laid the cat in a box before taking it to the vet the next day. A few hours later the vet rang to say that the cat had been chipped and its owners had taken it home to bury it. The cat was a boy called Nibbles and the vet had told me his owners were very grateful that their children had been able to say goodbye. They wanted to thank me for what I had done and I was glad I had been able to help. But as I heard what the vet said doubts filled me again. Was it time for George and me to say goodbye too? Could I really keep clinging to a hope that just kept getting stretched thinner with every day that passed?

I sat down in the front row of the church beside Mum, Boy and Sandra. We all went to our local Spiritualist church because Dad's mum, Edith, had been a Spiritualist and it was a bit of a tradition for our family. Dad's feet had been far too firmly on the ground to take us to a church where people spoke to those on the other side, but it had always been there in the background when we were kids and I knew Dad believed in life beyond death in his own quiet way. I'd started going regularly when I was about 17 and while religion isn't everyone's kind of thing, and a Spiritualist church might be to even fewer people's liking, I loved going there. It was one hour each week that was peaceful, and I liked seeing people find comfort as we celebrated life with singing and smiles.

But I wasn't sure if even church was going to make me feel any better today. I was here to pray for Ben's return, just as I did every week, but the night I'd found Nibbles was still fresh in my mind and I couldn't stop thinking about it. George was struggling so much with the rehearsals for this year's Christmas concert at Marjorie Kinnan that he kept running out of them, and we'd hardly had the TV on because it was so full of festive programs. George couldn't bear to hear Christmas even mentioned.

I couldn't help but think back to how happy we'd been last year, and I started crying quietly. I had never known it was possible to feel this lonely, as though I had an ache deep down in my bones, a sadness that could not be cured by sleep or talking. Of course I knew that I could phone my family any time of the day or night, but they had their own lives and I often had to deal by myself with my fears about what might happen to George if I did not find Ben.

I hardly noticed the service going on or the medium coming forward to talk to the congregation at the end of it, but when he pointed at me I had to listen.

"You with the white jumper," the medium said.

I looked around.

"Yes, you with the curly hair," he said to me.

Now you should know that every medium is different. Some see the shadows of spirits among the congregation, while others talk to them as though they're having a chat with a person. Messages aren't given out at every service, but I liked it when they were because there was such a feeling of peace in the room and a sense of comfort as people spoke to the ones they'd loved and lost. But I shifted uncomfortably in my seat as the medium looked into my eyes. I knew he would never be able to give me what I wanted, a postcode for the place where Ben was, because messages from the other side were never that exact.

"Things are going to change," the medium said in a deep voice. "Something beautiful is coming your way."

The man started moving his hands as he spoke.

"I can see a man. He's tall and handsome."

The medium rested his hands on his belly.

"He died from a long illness connected to the stomach."

I froze. Dad had died of pancreatitis.

"Heaven was the only place he had left," the medium said. "He didn't ever want to leave you but he's by your side now."

I didn't move a muscle and neither did Mum, Boy or Sandra, who were sitting with me.

"You have the same blue eyes as him," the medium said. "A lovely blue that shines when you smile."

I was the only one of the four of us with eyes the exact same shade as Dad's. Could this really be true? Was he really here with us now?

"That's better," the medium said as I smiled. "It brings him closer when you do that."

As I thought about Dad, I started crying again. I wanted to shout out, tell him that time was running out, that I had to find Ben before it was too late, and a rush of grief that we had lost Dad filled me, as raw as it was on the day when I first felt it.

The medium took a step back, looking at me.

"He's leaving now," he said. "But he wants you to know he's listening, so keep talking."

If Dad really was here, I knew what he was trying to tell me. For years, I'd chatted to him as I went about my days, telling him about what was going on as if he was still with us, and sometimes I could swear it felt as though he was. But I'd stopped doing it since Ben had gone, because I felt too sad to think about someone else that I'd loved and lost.

"He's dressing you all in pink," the medium told me. "You look like a doll."

The medium gave a great big laugh and so did Mum and Boy. They knew what that meant. Dad's nickname for me had always been "The Pink Princess', because I loved the color so much that I'd have dyed my hair and skin pink if I'd been allowed to.

The church went silent again as the medium sat down and I wondered about what had just happened. I felt calm now, almost peaceful.

"I'll always be with you," Dad had told me when I was a little girl and had been woken up by a bad dream or when I was a grown-up struggling to do the best for George.

As the service ended, I knew what Dad had been trying to tell me: he was with me every step of the way, keeping an eye on me just as he always had.

Now you might not believe in all this, you might think it's wrong to talk to the other side, but we all find strength in our own different ways, don't we? Faith means different things to different people, but I believe it's about what makes you smile inside, and I could smile again as I walked out into the cold. I had to keep believing. I could not give up on hope now I knew Dad was beside me.

Chapter 18

I ran to the phone like an Olympic sprinter when it rang on the morning of December 21. It was three months to the day since Ben had gone missing and I'd gotten more and more upset that in the past few days the calls had tailed off. I couldn't understand why people had stopped phoning until Mum told me they were all busy getting ready for Christmas.

"I think I've found your cat," I heard a woman say as I picked up the phone. "He's in my garden."

"Can I come over to look?"

"Sorry, but I'm leaving for my holiday in a minute. I'm going away for Christmas."

"Can't I just pop over quickly before you go?"

"No, love. My son's coming to get me, but I'll let you know when I get back."

The woman slammed down the phone and I stared around the room, wanting to scream. What if she really had found Ben? He'd be gone from her garden by the time she got home from Christmas. It really might be him and I'd lose him because she didn't want to be five minutes late for her holiday. Anger filled me as I sat down at the computer and logged on to the missing pet Web sites. Even the chat rooms, which were normally full of people, were quiet now. The world was shutting down for Christmas and I didn't want it to. I wanted everyone to keep searching just as I was.

But I couldn't ignore Christmas, however busy I kept myself. It was just four days away and I was dreading it. I didn't know how we were going to get through the day and I hadn't got a thing ready; but then again there was nothing to get ready because George and I were just going to have a quiet day. I knew that I'd breathe a huge sigh of relief when it was over, even though I hated the idea of starting a new year without Ben: it would feel as though time was moving on in such a concrete way.

The day dragged by and Howard was over to visit George when Wendy popped in at about 7:00 p.m. She came to see me each day, and although she didn't say as much, I knew she liked to check up on me and George. As patiently as ever, she would listen to me rambling on and take another pile of leaflets before telling me to get some rest and going home. She was the best kind of friend.

As we sat chatting, the phone rang again and I picked it up with a sigh. The woman from this morning had just about finished me off. I wasn't sure I could put up with another wild goose chase or a promise of hope that was soon dashed.

"I think I've found your cat," a woman said.

"Do you?" I asked, in the kind of voice I'd usually use for a two-year-old.

"Yes. I think so. Is your name Julia Romp?"

"Yes."

"Have you lost your cat?"

"Yes."

She must be daft. Everyone within a five-mile radius knew I'd lost my cat.

"And is your cat called Ben?"

"Yes."

"Well, he's in my conservatory."

"Really?" I sighed.

"Yes."

This was getting to me now. What was wrong with people?

"And where's your conservatory?"

"Brighton."

I nearly fell off the sofa. Brighton was 70 miles away. There was no way this woman could have seen a poster all the way down there.

"Brighton by the sea Brighton?"

"Yes. And you live in London? That's what the chip said. I got your phone number from it too."

I felt dizzy as she spoke.

"The chip?"

"Yes. My daughter, Carla, saw a cat sitting in our garden for several days. It kept coming back and she persuaded us to take him in. So a friend of mine who works at a cat rescue center came over with a microchip reader and that's how we got your details."

I could hardly hear what she was saying any more; I couldn't breathe as I listened and the blood rushed through my ears. She'd found a black and white cat that was micro-chipped with my details?

"Can I come and see you tonight?" I said in a rush, as Wendy stared at my white face.

"I'm not sure you'll get here," the woman said. "There's been heavy snow and the roads are closed."

I looked out of the window. There wasn't a snowflake to be seen in Hounslow. Was this woman having me on?

"Snow?" I said.

"Yes. Two foot deep."

I thought back to the news report I'd heard on the radio earlier that day as I'd done the washing up. Snowstorms and blizzards in parts of the country, people getting stuck in drifts and abandoning their cars—I hadn't really taken it all in then and I certainly couldn't now.

"I'll be there as soon as I can," I said.

"Well, if you're sure," the woman replied uncertainly. "It's a long drive."

"I'll leave now," I said and took down her address.

Wendy looked at me as I put down the phone and started jumping around the living room, scrabbling to get my hand-bag and car keys.

"I've got to go," I told her. "That woman said she had Ben in Brighton."

"Brighton?"

"Yes. I think it might really be him because she says the cat has got a chip with my details on it."

"Really?"

"Yes."

I grabbed my phone to text Mum, Tor, Boy and Nob to tell them what had happened. Howard could look after George and if I left now I'd get to Brighton by about 9:30 p.m. I was like a chicken with its head cut off as I rushed around.

Wendy looked at me. "I'm coming with you," she said.

"Are you sure?"

"Of course, Ju. You're not going alone. Are you OK?" Wendy asked.

"I think so."

But I wasn't sure. You see, as excited as I was, as concrete as all this sounded, there was still a doubt inside me. Could this really be Ben? After all these months and all my searching, was it really him? How on earth had he gotten to Brighton? It was miles away and Ben had been missing for so long. The woman sounded for real, but maybe this was a trick. If Ben really had been taken by someone, maybe they wanted to play one final joke before Christmas and had chipped another black and white cat with my details. I couldn't be sure until I saw it.

I ran upstairs to tell George I was going out.

"A woman's phoned," I said as I went into his room. "She thinks she's found Ben. I'm going to drive to the seaside to see."

He looked at me. "It's not him," he said. "It's another wrong cat."

I didn't want to get his hopes up too high, so I didn't say anything more. Maybe George was right. I couldn't go building him up just to knock him down again.

"Dad's going to stay with you and I'll be back as soon as I can," I said and rushed out of the room.

My hands were shaking so much as I got into my car that Keith had to type the address into the GPS for me before Wendy got into the passenger seat. We'd only got halfway down the road when my phone started ringing. I knew who it was: my family.

"Can you talk to them?" I said to Wendy.

Mum wanted to know if I was sure where I was going, Nob wanted to be certain there was someone with me and Boy wanted to ask if this was another bad joke. The one thing they were all agreed on, though, was that I'd never get to Brighton because of the snow.

"We'll be fine, won't we, Wend?" I said as we got on to the motorway.

She gave me a weak smile.

Soon the snow was coming down so thickly that the windscreen wipers could hardly get through it. I'd never known snow like it. I slowed the car down to about 30 mph as we crawled up the M3 before turning on to the M25. As soon as we got on to it, I realized just how bad things were. There were cars abandoned on the hard shoulder, others stuck in drifts. I crouched down over the steering wheel, determined to keep going. I had to get to Brighton. Not even a blizzard would stop me.

Wendy and I didn't chat, and I was concentrating on the road, but as I did so I couldn't stop thinking. Was this really Ben? How could it be? And if it was, where had he been for all this time? Even as I let myself dare to think it was and a picture of George and Ben together again appeared in my mind, I pushed it out. I could hardly believe that after all this time I might have finally found Ben—and so far away. I couldn't get rid of the feeling that this all might be another terrible trick that was being played on George and me.

It took us five hours to reach Brighton and the town was deserted when we arrived at around midnight. Everything was covered in a thick white blanket of snow as the sat nav told me we were getting close to the address and I did a right turn before it told me to take a final left. Wendy and I looked at each other as I turned the steering wheel. The woman on the phone had said she lived on a steep hill and she hadn't been exaggerating: it looked like Mount Everest stretching up ahead of us.

"Let's just take it slowly," Wendy said, and with that the car started sliding backward.

"Bloody thing!" I cried.

"It's not a Land Rover, Ju," Wendy told me. "It's not going to get up here."

"I'll try one more time."

But as the car skidded slowly across the road, I knew I had to give up trying. I found a parking space and got out in a complete daze, about to start walking up the hill.

"Have you locked the car, Ju?" Wendy called.

"No."

I turned around to go back and lock the car before starting up the hill again. The snow was halfway up my shins. I'd practically need ropes and an ice ax to get through it.

"Have you got the cat carrier, Ju?" said Wendy.

I hadn't. I went back to open the trunk and get it. Wendy took the carrier as I locked the car again and turned to start walking.

"Have you got the address?" Wendy asked.

I hadn't.

When we were finally ready, Wendy and I set off up the hill. Wendy seemed calm enough, but I was pretty sure she must be wishing by now that I'd disappear myself. The streetlight glinted off the snow as we started walking up the hill, but other than that the road was dark. No one had lit up their houses for Christmas here. It seemed strange, because I was so used to our estate. But as we got farther up the hill, we could see a house that was lit up. It was covered in lights that flashed color and warmth into the cold night, and as we counted down the house numbers, I realized it was the one we were looking for.

Wendy and I walked through a gate and stopped to stare silently. The house was covered in decorations just like the ones I'd used for our winter wonderland—a snowman, stars and bells—and lights were twinkling all over the house just as they had on mine this time last year.

"He came home for Christmas," I said to Wendy as we got to the door. "He chose this house because he recognized the lights."

I reached out to knock on the door but suddenly stopped my hand as a wave of panic rushed over me. I wasn't sure if I could bear another disappointment.

"I feel scared," I told Wendy.

"I know," she said, "but don't be."

I took a deep breath as fear and excitement flooded into me and I raised my hand to knock on the door.

A nice-looking man smiled at us and I could see a woman and a young girl standing in the hallway behind him.

"You must be Julia," he said. "Come in. I'm Steve and this is my wife, Alison, and our daughter, Carla."

They all looked so happy to see us, not seeming to mind that it was after midnight and two complete strangers had turned up demanding to see a mystery cat.

"Carla found him," Steve said, gesturing to his little girl. "She saw him sitting in our garden day after day, just staring into the house. He sat so still and for so long that the snow settled on him. He looked so miserable that Carla insisted we take him in. She's been like that since she was small: she's always the one to find lost pets."

Carla had blonde wavy hair and looked about 12. She was smiling fit to burst as the family dog, which was as big as a donkey, almost knocked me over.

"Do you want a drink?" Alison asked Wendy and me.

"No," I said nervously, hoping I didn't sound rude but unable to bear another minute of waiting. "I'd really like to see the cat."

"Of course," Steve said. "He's in the conservatory. We bought him a bed and put the heating on to make sure he was warm enough."

As Steve led us through the kitchen to the back of the house I could hardly put one foot in front of the other. My heart was beating so hard that I had pains in my chest. I didn't know what I'd do or say if it wasn't Ben. I was scared that I might just lie down on the floor and never get up again. It felt as though all the fear and hope, doubts and belief had rushed into this one moment.

We got to the conservatory and I looked through the glass door. There was a pet bed in the corner but no sign of a cat as Steve opened the door and I walked slowly into the room.

"Baboo?" I said, my voice shaking. "Benny Boo?"

I heard a noise as something moved in the cat bed and then a nose peeped out. It was black. My heart thumped even harder. The nose poked farther into the air and I saw a little bit of white fur underneath. It was shaped like a butterfly. I could hardly breathe. Then a black head appeared and I saw a white bib of fur on the cat's chest. Could it really be?

The cat turned its head toward me and all I could see was its eyes—huge, green and wise.

"Ben!" I sobbed as I dropped to my knees and he ran across the room toward me.

I opened my arms and it seemed like forever until Ben jumped into them. Then I felt the weight of him in my arms, his soft fur as it brushed my face, and knew he was real. Holding on to Ben as if I would never let him go, I could hardly believe I had found him. But his weight, the smell of him and the feel of his soft fur told me that I had. As Ben put his paws around my neck and nuzzled into me like a baby, I could feel the thickness of his coat and hear the sound of him purring like a lion as I started to cry.

"Baboo! Where have you been?"

Ben looked up at me again and my heart felt as though it was going to burst. All my hope and faith had been stretched so thin that I'd begun to wonder if I was wrong to believe in Ben as I did, in the love that would somehow bring us back together. Now I knew I'd been right to hope he'd come back to us. Ben was sitting in my arms, his paws clamped around me so hard I thought he'd never let go, and I swear he smiled as I looked at him with just one thought in my mind. George.

"Thank you," I said through my sobs to Steve, Carla and Alison, who were standing by the door. "Thank you so very much." I looked at Carla. "You can never know what you've done," I said. "I can't thank you enough."

I hugged Ben to me again and he meowed with pleasure as my tears fell on to his fur. If finding Ben was a Christmas miracle, Carla was the Christmas fairy who'd made it happen. As Ben purred she smiled at me again. He was safe and sound—just as we all would be now we had found him. My search was finally over. All I had to do now was get home to George.

You wouldn't believe the drive home we had. All I wanted was to get back as quickly as possible, because I didn't want George to be apart from Ben for another minute. But when Wendy asked the GPS to give us the quickest route back to London, rather than the easiest one, it directed me down every country lane in Sussex and we got completely lost. We met people with shovels ready to dig themselves through the snowdrifts, others who'd broken down and a policeman who wondered what on earth we were doing trying to drive my tiny car through the snowy wilderness. All the while, Ben was meowing in the cat carrier on the backseat, and I felt awful that I was putting him through another adventure when his last one had only just ended.

Wendy and I couldn't stop talking about it all as I drove. Where had Ben been all this time? He certainly looked too well fed to have been fending for himself for three months. How had he got down the motorway to Brighton, and who had been looking after him? He couldn't have gotten all that way alone, surely, so had someone taken him? But as Wendy and I talked about it during the long drive home I realized that I would never know for sure. It was going to be a mystery that would never be solved; but it didn't matter, because Ben was home and that was all I'd ever wanted.

Hours later, we finally got back to Hounslow and I was filled with nerves as Wendy gave me a smile before opening her front door. As I walked into my house, I felt almost dazed. It was 4:00 a.m. but I knew George wouldn't be asleep. I could hear my heart thumping in my ears as I took Ben out of the carrier and stood at the bottom of the stairs with him in my arms.

"George?" I called. "He's home. Ben's home."

I heard footsteps and George's face appeared at the top of the stairs. He looked unsure, almost scared.

"He's here, George. Ben is really here. I've found him. He's come home."

George flew down the stairs before stopping suddenly as he got to the last step. He stared at Ben, who was looking around, as if shocked to be back in the home he'd left so long before. Then he looked at George and their eyes locked together, one set green, one set blue, as they stared at each other.

"Baboo!" George cried. "Where have you been?"

"He's been on holiday," I said in my cat voice. "He's been to the sea. He was very tired in the car but he's fine now."

George didn't speak or take Ben from my arms. He just stood and stared at us as if he could hardly believe that Ben was real. It was as if George could not let himself believe that his friend was home again after so long wishing and hoping. My heart quivered as he turned away from me.

But then George carefully laid himself down on the floor and looked up at me. Gently, I put Ben down and he stared around before taking a step toward his friend, stopping to sniff the air, moving step by step toward him. George just gazed at Ben and I saw peace in his eyes for the first time since that awful day when Ben had gone missing. He stayed completely still as Ben bent down to smell him, his face, his hair, his clothes, before climbing on to his chest and lying down. Time stopped as George put his arms around Ben and started to stroke him.

"You've been to the sea?" he said, his voice high and curling, full of love and tenderness again. "You've been surfing and on a boat, haven't you? I know you have."

I waited, wondering if that was all he'd say in cat talk for now. George was quiet for a minute before looking at Ben and my heart leaped as the words tumbled out of him.

"Did you bring me a bucket of sand home? Did you go swimming? There's fish and chips at the sea. Did you have ketchup with them? Did you see Katie Price? She lives in Brighton. Did you see fishes—lots of lovely fishes? Or were you a pirate on a big ship? I think you were out on the wide blue sea and that's why you've only just come home. It is, isn't it? You've been away at sea."

The words danced in the air between us as I looked at George with Ben.

"You're a beach bum, Baboo!" George said with a giggle. "You used a bucket and spade. The beach is pebbly at Brighton, isn't it? Did the boat have a horn? Did you go on the sea and look at the fishes?"

He carried on talking, laughing as he stroked Ben and hugged him, the love pouring out of him just as it always had done.

"He's been living with a girl called Carla," I said.

"Have you?" George asked Baboo.

"Yes. It was like a hotel. He had a nice warm bed and there were lights on the house just like ours."

For a moment, George's face darkened. "I don't want to talk about it," he said. "Let's not talk about it ever again. Ben's home now. He's home with us. He's never going to leave us again."

He leaned forward to give Ben a kiss, digging his fingers into his fur as he cuddled him. Ben purred in delight before jumping off George's chest and on to the floor, where he crouched down over his paws, staring up at his friend.

Come on, George. Let's play! I'm home now. I'm back and I've missed you so very much.

With that, he ran upstairs and George went after him.

"We're going to play hide and seek," he called as he went up the stairs. "Ben loves being home, Mum, doesn't he?"

"Yes, George. I think he does."

"I do too."

George ran off up the stairs and I could hear him laughing as he played with Ben. A feeling of peace filled me. George had come to life again in the moment that he saw Ben, just as I'd always thought he would. He had finally come back to me, we were together again and in the instant that Ben came home all the sadness of the past three months had disappeared. As I walked into the kitchen to put the kettle on, I stared out at the dark sky as I waited for the water to boil and listened to George's laughter. The sweetest sound.

Then I heard his footsteps running down the stairs and he ran into the kitchen.

"Can we get the decorations out, Mum?" he asked. "And the tree? Ben wants Christmas to start now."

"Yes, but I haven't got a thing ready," I said with a laugh. "There's no special food in the fridge or presents under the tree."

"It doesn't matter," George said. "You can wrap up the toys from last year like I'm always telling you."

He ran off again and I turned to follow him. Ben was home, we were together and as I got to the top of the stairs the two of them were waiting for me. I started laughing as Ben dashed into my bedroom, jumped on the bed and careened off it like a rocket. He was just as excited as George and I were.

"Mum?" George said as I stood on the landing and wondered how on earth we were going to get everything ready in time.

"Yes, George?"

"I think this is going to be the best Christmas ever."

"Really?"

"Yes."

Epilogue

As George decorated the Christmas tree and Ben scampered around as if he'd never been away, I started thinking
about all that had happened—the tears and doubts, sleep-
less nights and worrying. And as I looked at George and
Ben together, I was sure of something I'd never been certain
of before. Ever since George had been born, I'd never quite
gotten rid of the feeling that I had failed him by not giving
him a proper family, a mum and dad who were married and
the kind of childhood that I'd had and loved so much. But
when Ben went missing, I had finally realized that George
did have a family. Just because it was a different shape and
size from the one I'd known didn't make it less of one. Ben,
George and I were a family and we were complete.

A year on, we are still in Hounslow and life has slipped
back to how it should be: George has turned 14 and goes to
school, and we talk, laugh and play together with Ben, who
spends the rest of the time sunning himself in the

summerhouse or chasing off dogs. The moment he got home again, our life together became what it had once been. George started cuddling me again and talking about love. He mentions it more and more often now, either telling me he loves me as we joke together or saying that Ben loves me. Each time he does, I know how lucky I am to hear those words.

As for me? Well, I'm still an almost pet detective. A few days after Ben got home, I got a phone call from a woman in Devon whose cat, Numpty, had disappeared when she and her family had been to Hounslow for Christmas with her mum and taken him with them. The woman had found out about me because her mum had one of my posters on her fridge.

"Where do I start?" she said. "I have to go home in two days and I don't know how I'm going to find him."

How could I say no when I'd only just got Ben home and the memory of the pain of being without him was still so fresh inside me? I told the woman I'd do what I could.

"It's good you're helping, because Numpty's family is probably crying like we were," George told me as I printed posters. "They'll be sad."

It took me nine weeks to find Numpty, but I did in the end. He'd been found wandering by an elderly couple who'd been feeding him and they recognized his picture on one of my new posters. I found Numpty lazing on the sofa as though he was in a five-star hotel.

At the moment I'm looking for Samba, in between helping out at animal charities by taking cats to appointments with the vet or inspecting homes to see if they're suitable for a pet. I like doing it and I know I'll keep on searching for cats when people lose them, because I understand what they mean to those who love them. Our life changed the moment we lost Ben—just as it did when he came home again—and I still remind myself to thank the family who helped him finally get home to us again.

So now I've told you our story, there is someone else who'd like to tell you a bit about himself and Ben.

Ben likes food and treats. He loves being with me if I try to bounce. He gets on the trampoline. If I play computer, he sits on my lap and eats Cheerios out of my bowl. He even wants to eat when I do. Ben can't lie. He loves us all the time. He is never sad. But sometimes he likes to bite my mum. I love it. It's funny. He likes to be naughty like me. Ben is kind and loves me touching him. He purrs. He loves to be with me all the time and I do cat talk with Ben so he don't feel left out. It's fun and I love chasing him and when I call him he runs away. It's funny. When I do cat talk, I get happy and excited. Cat talk makes me and my mum and Ben feel close. It makes me happy and we love all the adventures Ben goes on. My mum tells me stories about him and I tell better ones. Mum's are funny.

When Ben went missing, I thought he was dead. Just dead, gone. I don't know why just dead. My mum looked for him and people phoned and made my mum cry. It was like an empty house. I didn't have anyone to play with and I was in my room missing him. Tears come out my eyes and they hurt when I thought he was gone. Every day when I got on my bus Mum said this:

"Don't worry. I will be out all day looking for Ben." I missed talking to him and every day I woke up he was not in his chair. It's so good he's home now. He makes me comfortable.

The things I like are:

Xbox—It's good talking to people I can't see. I wouldn't like to see them. Some are 11 and some are 55. I like it when they say I'm good. They think I'm a really normal kid. I don't tell anyone I have special needs. They would laugh at me. But sometimes I spell things wrong. I called someone a beast but I meant best and they called me stupid. But I'm a better player.

School—At first I did not like it because I did not know the people around me or the teachers. It took me a while to get used to them and I didn't look at anyone or try to talk. I didn't like the chairs. They make you sit straight and I still don't like them or the uniform or the smell of school dinners. But I love my school and I want to stay there as long as possible. My school is the happiest place to be.

Shiny earrings, water and swimming, sweets that last for a long time, London Aquarium, making mince pies because I make them lovely, animal documentaries, magnets, orange chocolate.

Knowing the time so I know how many hours I have.

My bed, but I don't like going to sleep.

The things I don't like are:

Liars.

People who pull faces when they look at you.

Shouting makes me worried.

Small rooms.

People who smell of Wotsits or coffee.

Jokes because I can't understand them and people make them and I can't work them out.

My mum when she looks down and breathes loud or when she don't answer if I talk and she says she's thinking.

When people say "You look happy" because Mum says they say it when I'm not smiling and I feel happy inside but people still say that.

I know I act different sometimes. I try to fit in and it don't work and it makes me sad. I would never cry or show my feelings at school. People don't understand me. I want to look and talk but it don't come out and it comes out wrong. If I'm happy inside, I can't smile. I don't like showing it in case I look over the top. Lots of people have laughed at me and it makes me feel sad. But my mum will tell me how good I am at everything and I'm special. My mum makes me feel good. She says we are all different and have a bit of all sorts inside us. I tell the truth but sometimes it hurts people's feelings. Mum said we need to think before we say something and I'm much better at that now. Not that I need my mum to figure this out for me.

Here are the people I know:

Michelle—She smelled nice of washing powder and made me happy. She would say "Do you want a drink, George?" She had pictures all over her flat of Ricky and Ashley when they was little. Michelle only liked trainers. She had five pairs. She liked jeans and ate toast.

Arthur—He was my friend and every day he knocked for me. We played football or trampoline. His mum was small and their dog Jedi dribbled.

Nanny Zena—She's my dad's mum and she made me a clown teddy when she used to knit. Now she is blind and can't knit any more.

Nanny Carol—She's my mum's mum and held me first when I was born. She is an old pensioner who has a bus pass and she is going to start living like a teenager now she has a bus pass. She loves cakes with cream. She can eat a whole birthday cake.

Dad—He takes me swimming and plays computer games like I do.

Lewis—He's kind, lovely and a good dancer. Mum says to him, "Look after George, won't you?" when we go out but it's the other way round because I have to look after him.

Nob—He's strict but kind.

Boy—He's laid back.

Sandra—She's always having a baby.

Tor—She looks like my mum but different.

Dell—He's Tor's husband and he's Mr. Cool.

Wendy—Her face stays the same every day. She doesn't change. She says "Hello George."

My mum—Before Ben came, I didn't want to love anyone. I didn't know what love was. I didn't think about it really. I just remember knowing my mum was there to look after me. But it's different now.

That's just a little bit about George. There's so much more to him and Ben is the one who helped him show it all to the world. This isn't the story of a magic cure for autism, of course, but it is our story about the magic that Ben gave George by bringing out his playfulness, fun and most of all love. Ben changed our lives forever and while George will always struggle in many ways, I believe the love he has for Ben—and the way it helped to bring George and me so much closer together—saved us both. If Ben was taken for a reason, it was to show us how powerful the love inside George is, because without Ben, he was lost. With him, he has a center, a voice and a way to show the world all the good inside him.

Losing Ben made me realize that I have to prepare for the day when he leaves us for good and is too old or ill to stay with George anymore. So I have started mentioning to George that one day Ben might have a kitten and he seems convinced that it's possible, because anything is when it comes to Ben. One day in the not-too-distant future, I will bring a kitten home and tell George that it is Ben's son or daughter. I hope he will learn to fall in love with it just as he did Ben.

For now, I focus on each day as it comes. Some are harder than others but throughout them all, I am so proud of George and all he has achieved—reading and writing, caring for his classmates and being a loving boy who cares about the world and people around him. I can honestly say that George really is the best son a mother could ask for and I love everything about the person he is. He's truly unique, and that's just about as much as any mother could want.

Acknowledgments

My most special thanks must go to Mum, Tor, Nob, Boy, Lewis and the rest of my family: you put up with my schemes, love and support me every step of the way and I couldn't be without you.

To all the people who have helped George in the past and continue to do so today—Andy Leigh, Wendy Vogel, Michael Schlesinger, Miss Proctor, Ms. Bahsin, Mr. Classon and Mr. Thurman—and everyone at Marjorie Kinnan—Mrs. Adams, Mrs. Ward, Mrs. Nagel and all the rest of the staff—you make George's world a much happier place.

It would be impossible to name everyone who helped me search for Ben but every phone call and message of support, whether from a stranger or a friend, was so appreciated. Special mention must go to Wendy, Keith, Nikki and Kayleigh; Alison, Steve and Carla; Tracy, Anne and Eliza; the staff at the Animal Rescue Center in Twickenham; Norma Mackie; Pat Cole and Jessica Thompson at the *Hounslow Chronicle*.

Thanks also to Mavis, Monty and Socks—I know how much you miss Prudence.

And finally a big thank-you to Laetitia Rutherford, for finding me; all at HarperCollins for believing in my story; and Megan Lloyd Davies for helping me laugh while I told it.